REKINDLING AN
OLD LIGHT

THE VIRTUE AND VALUE OF
CHRIST-SHAPED LIBERAL ARTS LEARNING

R. KEITH LOFTIN

HIGH BRIDGE BOOKS
HOUSTON

Rekindling an Old Light
by R. Keith Loftin

Copyright © 2022 by R. Keith Loftin
All rights reserved.

Printed in the United States of America
ISBN: 978-1-954943-60-5

All rights reserved. Except in the case of brief quotations embodied in critical articles and reviews, no portion of this book may be reproduced, stored in a retrieval system, or transmitted in any form or by any means—electronic, mechanical, photocopy, recording, scanning, or other—without prior written permission from the author.

Scripture quotations marked NET are from the NET Bible® https://netbible.com copyright ©1996, 2019 used with permission from Biblical Studies Press, L.L.C. All rights reserved".

Scripture quotations marked ESV are from The ESV® Bible (The Holy Bible, English Standard Version®). ESV® Text Edition: 2016. Copyright © 2001 by Crossway, a publishing ministry of Good News Publishers. The ESV® text has been reproduced in cooperation with and by permission of Good News Publishers. Unauthorized reproduction of this publication is prohibited. All rights reserved.

Scripture quotations marked NIV are from THE HOLY BIBLE, NEW INTERNATIONAL VERSION®, NIV® Copyright © 1973, 1978, 1984, 2011 by Biblica, Inc.® Used by permission. All rights reserved worldwide.

High Bridge Books titles may be purchased in bulk for educational, business, fundraising, or sales promotional use. For information, please contact High Bridge Books via www.HighBridgeBooks.com/contact.

Published in Houston, Texas by High Bridge Books in collaboration with Moral Apologetics Press and the Center for the Foundation of Ethics at Houston Christian University.

HOUSTON BAPTIST UNIVERSITY

CENTER *for the* FOUNDATIONS *of* ETHICS

The Center for the Foundations of Ethics at Houston Baptist University and Moral Apologetics Press are devoted to exploring the evidential significance of a range of moral realities—from the sacredness of life to the value and uniqueness of people, from the dignity of persons to their essential equality, from inviolable human rights to ubiquitous signals of transcendence, from authoritative moral obligations to the possibility of moral knowledge, from the need for moral forgiveness and transformation to the rational stability of the ethical enterprise.

CONTENTS

ABOUT THE
CONTRIBUTORS

Marybeth Baggett (PhD, Indiana University of Pennsylvania) is Professor of English and Cultural Apologetics at Houston Christian University.

Timothy E. G. Bartel (PhD, University of St. Andrews) is Provost and Professor of Great Texts and Writing at The College at the Saint Constantine School in Houston, Texas.

Travis Dickinson (PhD, University of Iowa) is Professor of Philosophy at Dallas Baptist University.

Paul M. Gould (PhD, Purdue University) is Associate Professor of Philosophy and Director of the M.A. in Philosophy of Religion program at Palm Beach Atlantic University.

Mark D. Janzen (PhD, University of Memphis) is Associate Professor of Archeology at Lipscombe University.

David Lyle Jeffrey (PhD, Princeton University) is Distinguished Professor of Literature and the Humanities at Baylor University.

R. Keith Loftin (PhD, University of Aberdeen) is Professor of Philosophy and Director of the Politics, Philosophy, Economics program at Dallas Baptist University.

Stephen D. Mizell (PhD, Southwestern Baptist Theological Seminary) is a middle school literature and composition teacher at Great Hearts Academy in Arlington, TX.

Melinda Nielsen (PhD, University of Notre Dame) is Associate Professor of Classical Literature at Baylor University.

Greg Peters (PhD, University of Toronto) is Professor of Medieval and Spiritual Theology at Biola University's Torrey Honors Institute.

John Mark Reynolds (PhD, University of Rochester) is President of The Saint Constantine School in Houston, Texas.

Hannah Rogers earned her Bachelor of Arts degree from Baylor University's University Scholars program, with concentrations in Classics and Literature. She is currently a doctoral student in literature at the University of Dallas.

Robert M. Sloan (Doktor der Theologie, University of Basel) is President of Houston Christian University.

FOREWORD

WRITING THE FOREWORD TO A BOOK OF THIS
sort usually presents a challenge in that collections of essays often do not hold together well. When that occurs, there is little to do but point to a few exceptional essays that stand out in their own right and commend their merit. This collection edited by Keith Loftin, however, is remarkable not only for the excellence of the individual pieces but for its thematic coherence.

Current discussions about the liberal arts struggle with two foundational issues: defining them and justifying their need with respect to educational curricula and the marketplace. Put another way, why do we need the liberal arts? What good are they, and can they help the student get a job?

The essays collected here develop these basic issues of defining and justifying the liberal arts from varying content angles (especially different academic disciplines) and do so in a way that—no doubt because of good editorial leadership—has made the project a success in describing the liberal arts and the value of preserving them. In short, this book is a resounding commendation of Christ-shaped liberal arts colleges and universities as places where students can get something more than an education that leads to a job. Such institutions can guide and mentor students in what it means to be truly human—living as a virtuous person under the authority of God (as revealed in Holy Scripture) and being thus shaped and prepared to do God's will and work in the world.

Toward this end of participating in God's restorative purposes for the world, the readers are exhorted, as imaginative and dramatic subcreators, to study the liberal arts (skills and practices that lead to freedom and thereby engender *humanitas*—human-ness) as a historic means of cultivating virtue and, in Christian terms, Christlikeness.

Studying the liberal arts begins—as this collection of essays so beautifully maintains—with submission to the authority of God and has the purpose of creating Christ-shaped humanness via reading and hearing great texts under the wise tutelage of informed mentors. Christian professors can coach their students toward entry into the great conversations of human experience and thereby promote living wisely and even dramatically as a way of "bodying forth" (incarnating in character and behavior) virtue and wisdom. Such Christ-shaped humanness involves being prepared to adapt to the changes of a fallen world—with all of its unruly galloping and lurching—but nonetheless living faithfully under the superintending hand of God.

I close with reference to those to whom I commend this volume. It was no doubt intended for prospective college students and their parents, those who need to make important decisions about the kind of university they will choose—Christian or otherwise. Certainly high school students and those who influence them will find great benefit, even guidance, in these essays.

But I also strongly encourage the reading of this volume by college professors of every discipline who seek to serve Christ. The liberal arts are indeed being lost in our age, and we need to remember the "what" and the "why" of them—what they are and why we should retain them. I also commend this work to university administrators, those who, in spite of their sincere devotion to Christ, have lost—by ignorance or forgetfulness—the historic sense of what the university is for, what a Christian university can do (and recover), and why a Christ-shaped commitment to the liberal arts is important.

There need be, given the deteriorating discourse and curricular habits of current academic culture, no great shame in not knowing what the liberal arts are, but there is shame in refusing to (re-)learn those practices, thus jeopardizing our distinctive mission as Christian universities: our Lord Christ is the very image of God, and to be fully human is to be like him. Or to put it more comprehensively, God is at work in the world to restore our full human-ness in Christ (Col. 3:10), which surely should be among the goals of a Christian university.

—**Robert M. Sloan**
President, Houston Christian University

1

AN INVITATION TO CHRIST-SHAPED LIBERAL EDUCATION

R. Keith Loftin

JULY 1916 SAW J. R. R. TOLKIEN ON THE FRONT-lines of the ongoing Battle of the Somme, one of the truly pivotal actions of World War I. Tolkien, who became one of the 20th century's most prominent literary figures as the author of *The Lord of the Rings*, had been deployed in France for just over a month when he learned that his dear friend Robert Gilson had been killed in action. The sudden loss of Gilson's friendship prompted Tolkien to reflect on the purpose of his life, as well as that of his small circle of friends. He believed his group "was destined to testify for God and Truth." They were, he wrote, "destined to kindle a new light, or, what is the same thing, rekindle an old light in the world."[1]

What is this "old light," and why and how is it to be "rekindled"? The answers to these questions were, for Tolkien and his friends, bound up with their shared sense of vocation and meaning. Tolkien and his friends wished to awaken in modern man the sense of *enchantment*. They sought to reillumine the truth, beauty, and goodness of the world through story and poetry. Tolkien and company perceived this work as their contribution to the *flourishing* of others. Men and women flourish when they live the life God intends for them. They flourish when their lives reflect God's *purpose* for humanity.

This book is about a certain type of college education, an education committed—like Tolkien—to re-kindling the old light, that is, to shaping students into flourishing persons who are prepared for lives of meaning, purpose, and virtue. This is Christ-shaped liberal education, or what is the same thing: Christian liberal arts education.

Surprisingly, many students and their parents never consider Christian liberal arts colleges as live options. Why? Largely, it seems, because they aren't familiar with the vision of Christ-shaped liberal education. They simply don't know what Christian liberal arts colleges *do* or what liberal education even *is*. This short book is for these students and their parents. The following chapters individually describe some of the main contours of a Christian liberal arts education. Certainly we're not attempting to say everything worth saying about the liberal arts. Our purpose is to convey the vision of Christ-shaped liberal education with an eye toward persuading readers that such education promises more, far more, than they might've originally expected.

Today's marketplace of higher education teems with competing visions of value and purpose. If you're an upperclassman in high school, odds are good your mailbox (not to mention your email inbox) is stuffed daily with ads and invitations to attend various colleges. The process of selecting a college can be bewildering. But it can also be exciting and deeply edifying, especially for Christians whose faith informs their decision-making. How might your faith inform the way you think about college education? The answer, I think, begins with the idea that people flourish when their lives reflect God's purpose for humanity.

BEGINNING WITH PREREQUISITES: SETTING THE HORIZON FOR COLLEGE EDUCATION

What is God's purpose for humanity? I've always found Augustine's summary of Christianity's answer helpful: the purpose of humanity is to live together in ordered harmony unto the Lord.[2] Our purpose is to *fit into* God's created order and to delight in doing so. Indeed, our purpose is to participate in God's intention for all of creation, a notion expressed in the biblical word *shalom.* As Cornelius Plantinga explains:

The webbing together of God, humans, and all creation in justice, fulfillment, and delight

> is what the Hebrew prophets call *shalom.* We call it peace, but it means far more than mere peace of mind or a cease-fire between enemies. In the Bible, shalom means *universal flourishing, wholeness, and delight*—a rich state of affairs in which natural needs are satisfied and natural gifts fruitfully employed, a state of affairs that inspires joyful wonder as its Creator and Savior opens doors and welcomes the creatures in whom he delights. Shalom, in other words, is the way things ought to be.[3]

God's desire, in short, is that men and women flourish. Flourishing (or "blessed") lives, we are told in Psalms 1 and 2, belong to those who "find pleasure in obeying the LORD'S commands" and who "take shelter in him" (NET). Shalom is the life, truly, wherein our deepest longings find satisfaction. Surely this is the life all parents desire for their children! As Christians, God's purpose shapes the horizon for how we think about college. God's intention and God's desire is that our lives be characterized by shalom. It is that we be humans *correctly.*

In Genesis 3, however, the intimacy and communion that characterized mankind's relationship with God were broken because of sin. Sin disrupts God's shalom. Things now are *not* the way they are supposed to be. Not only has sin estranged us from God, it also has distorted our relationships with one another. It has broken the harmony between man and the rest of the created order. It has left our inner lives disordered and unwhole. Sin also has misdirected us from our proper, God-given purposes.[4] If we hope to flourish, each of these must be set right. "You can get the idea," C. S. Lewis explains, "if you think of us as a fleet of ships" and our lives together as a joint voyage.

> The voyage will be a success only, in the first place, if the ships do not collide and get in one another's way; and, secondly, if each ship is seaworthy and has her engines in good order. As a matter of fact, you cannot have either of these two things without the other. If the ships keep on having collisions they will not remain seaworthy very long. On the other hand, if their steering gears are out of order they will not be able to avoid collisions. ... And however well the fleet sailed, its voyage would be a failure if it were meant to reach New York and actually arrived in Calcutta.[5]

With this horizon of God's shalom and human flourishing in view, we may say that Christ-shaped liberal education is education *for life*—for the life we are meant to have.

We cannot, of course, expect to flourish by accident. We could no more blunder into a state of flourishing than we could become a true friend through carelessness and self-centeredness. It requires intentional dedication. As Aristotle explains, flourishing likewise does not come overnight, and it has little to do with material wealth.[6] The point is not to minimize the importance of meeting physical needs and providing for one's family, but a life focused primarily on making money is a life at odds with shalom. It need hardly be added that no one, including the most loving of parents, can flourish on behalf of another. Each student must take responsibility for his or her own flourishing, and this realization must inform the way students and their parents approach the task of deciding upon college education.

Christ-shaped liberal education aims to cultivate students' flourishing, which just is their growth into Christlikeness. Jesus Christ is, after all, the quintessential human being. Jesus is the one "in whom are hidden all the treasures of wisdom and knowledge" (Colossians 2:3, NET). Jesus is "the primary Christian moral exemplar, the perfect embodiment of the human *telos* [purpose]."[7] If we wish to know what being a human correctly looks like, then we must look to Jesus. We are made to relate properly to God. We are, in other words, to "put on the Lord Jesus Christ" (Romans 13:14, NET). As C. S. Lewis notes, "It is not simply that God has arbitrarily made us such that He is our only good. Rather God is the only good of all creatures: and by necessity, each must find its good in that kind and degree of the fruition of God which is proper to its nature," in our case *human* nature.[8]

This means we live the truly good life when we live *in* Christ and when we are *like* Christ. Jesus is, to be sure, the "second Adam" (Romans 5:12-21) through whom men and women may be redeemed into God's shalom. Jesus is, certainly, the Son of God who "came to seek and to save the lost" (Luke 19:10, NET). We must appreciate what this means for our lives here and now: Jesus has come so that we "may have life, and may have it abundantly" (John 10:10, NET). This life, the flourishing life, includes our relationships with others, our values, our hobbies, our worship, our education, our jobs—indeed, *all* aspects of life. These principles of Christ and Christlikeness form the mainstay of Christ-shaped liberal education.

DECIDING TO MAJOR IN FLOURISHING: EDUCATION FOR SHALOM

Though anyone desiring truly to flourish must grow into Christ-likeness, we all are unique individuals. Unity is not, after all, uniformity. Although Christlikeness is God's general will for all of us, this does not mean that God desires to reduce us into some bland uniformity. Christ-shaped liberal education does not demand that all Christian students must declare the same major or embark on identical careers. Quite the contrary, in fact.

Students and their parents sometimes assume that Christian liberal arts colleges are only for students whose calling is to become pastors or missionaries or the like. Christian liberal arts colleges are not—so the assumption goes—worthwhile options for students destined to become accountants, electricians, nurses, engineers, therapists, for example. This assumption, however, is far from true. It is a misconception built on two significant mistakes, beginning with the mistake of dividing vocations into the "sacred" versus the "secular."

There are, it is true, Christian colleges that operate according to the so-called "Christian service" model. As Nicholas Wolterstorff explains, these schools believe the task of "Christian collegiate education" to be the training of "students to enter Christian service, understanding this to be a certain range of 'Christian' occupations or 'Kingdom work'—evangelism, church education, church ministry, mission-field medicine, Christian communications, and the like."[9] Whatever the value of such schools, they are not Christian liberal arts colleges. Whatever the value of such training, it is not Christ-shaped liberal education. To be sure, it's wonderful when God calls people to the pastorate or the mission field, and there can be no doubt that a Christ-shaped liberal education would be of tremendous value to these students. The assumption, however, that these occupations are *sacred* (or *real* "Kingdom work") whereas other vocations—such as accounting, factory work, nursing, engineering—are merely *secular* (or disconnected from God's purposes) is false. Our individual callings—our vocations—are *whatever* God would have each of us do toward fulfilling His purposes for humanity.

The Christian life, including your vocation or career, cannot properly be divided into sacred versus secular. Tellingly, this realization is what prompted the 16th century Christian reformer Martin Luther to insist that "tailors, cobblers, stonemasons, carpenters, cooks, innkeepers, farmers and all the temporal craftsmen" have been "consecrated" to "the work and office of his trade" just as pastors and missionaries have been to their offices.[10] We must remember that God called Nehemiah to work on the city walls of Jerusalem no less than he called Ezra to serve in the temple. We reject the mistaken "sacred" versus "secular" thinking, and in this book we present some of the excellent reasons for students from across the full spectrum of career aims to consider a college whose curriculum and ethos embody Christ-shaped liberal education.

Seeing through the false idea that there are "sacred" versus "secular" parts of life is important. It's important because it opens our eyes to the deep value of Christ-shaped liberal education for students planning to enter the workforce. It's important because it highlights the mistake in tacitly assuming that Christian liberal arts colleges are not worthwhile options because they offer the "wrong kind of education" for these students. Underlying that assumption, however, is confusion about the purpose of liberal education.

It's not surprising, in one sense, that confusion about the purpose of liberal arts education is so widespread. For starters, what passes for "liberal arts" courses at many of America's highest profile colleges and universities are little more than seminars promoting social agendas and ideologies that undermine human flourishing and shalom. Notwithstanding their prevalence, such courses are *pseudo* liberal arts courses masquerading as genuine liberal education, and they should hardly be confused with the pursuit of truth, beauty, and goodness (never mind shalom). Given this reality, thoughtful students and their parents may wonder whether Christian liberal arts colleges are any different. My hope is that the chapters in this book will relieve these concerns.

For many students and their parents, the well has been poisoned by the familiar tendency of talking heads to deprecate the liberal arts as the holdover of a bygone age, as irrelevant to practical concerns, or as only for those students who are "academically adrift" having frankly no idea what else to do ("I haven't decided on a major, so for now I'm just in liberal studies"). Before deciding to bypass Christian liberal arts colleges when making campus visits, however, students and their parents should ask themselves (and together have a discussion about) this fundamental question: *what is the point of collegiate education?* College is, of course, goal-directed, but amazingly many students and their parents never actually discuss their goal. So, what's your goal with college? Or perhaps more fittingly, how do you understand the connection between college education and God's desire that you flourish?

It is widely assumed that the point of attending college is to receive preparation for landing a job upon graduation. According to this thinking, the driving questions are *What can I do with this degree?* or *What can this degree do* for *me?* Christ-shaped liberal education, on the other hand, asks a more fundamental question: *What will this education do* to *me?* or perhaps more clearly *Who can I become with Christ-shaped liberal education?*

Don't misunderstand me here: the truth is that Christ-shaped liberal education is deeply concerned with your future vocation. There are several reasons for this, beginning with the fact that God created humans to be workers (like Him). This means our working ultimately is tied to God's intention for us.[11] Further, your vocation is an important aspect of how you participate in and contribute to a life of ordered harmony with others. And perhaps most importantly, you do not, upon driving into work each day, cease be a *human person* and turn into a mindless drone. Among the priorities of Christ-shaped liberal education are the cultivation of wisdom, the ability to think critically, virtue in interacting with others, and the invaluable skill of knowing how to learn. What could be more worthwhile both for flourishing and for holding down a career?

SEEKING EDUCATION FOR LIFE: CHRIST-SHAPED LIBERAL EDUCATION

Landing a good job is valuable and noble. A considerable portion of your adult life, after all, will be spent at work. Our society, though, has mistakenly conflated the "professional life" (or one's career) with life *itself*. Society has replaced human flourishing with financial success as life's purpose, and along the way it supplanted education with professional training as the means of succeeding. College planning by many families has been reduced to a cost-benefit analysis of (often astronomically high) tuition costs over against anticipated salaries. But your career is not the totality of your life. Flourishing cannot be measured in dollars.

The classical tradition of liberal arts education, of which Christian liberal arts colleges are inheritors, purposes to shape students' inner selves. The aim of this tradition, therefore, is preparation for all of life. Liberal arts education seeks the formation of your soul to perceive aright the truth, beauty, and goodness characteristic of the good life, and indeed the development of the skills and virtue necessary for flourishing.

This education is called "liberal" not because it is somehow connected with or oriented toward political liberalism (it isn't, by the way) but because it derives from the Latin word for "free" (*liber*). Professor Robert George's summary is spot on:

> According to the classic liberal-arts ideal, our critical engagement with great thinkers enriches our

understanding and enables us to grasp, or grasp more fully, great truths—truths that, when we appropriate them into our lives, liberate us from what is merely vulgar, coarse, or base. These soul-shaping, humanizing truths—truths whose appreciation and secure possession elevates reason above passion or appetite, enabling us to direct our desires and our will to what is truly good, truly beautiful, truly worthy of human beings as possessors of a profound and inherent dignity. The classical liberal-arts proposition is that intellectual knowledge has a role to play in making self-transcendence possible. It can help us to understand what is good and to love what is good above whatever it is we happen to desire; it can teach us to desire what is good because it is good, thus making us truly *masters of ourselves.*[12]

The idea is that liberal arts education contributes to freeing you from the tyranny of a disordered soul, from the limitations of parochialism, and from the indignity of being enslaved to your base desires.

Christ-shaped liberal education may be helpfully thought of, then, as a quest for value and purpose. All colleges and universities are organized, of course, on the basis of some perceived value. In fact, all human action is performed on the basis of some perceived value. Why do I awaken at 5:30 a.m.? To go to work. Why do I go to work? To receive a paycheck. Why do I desire a paycheck? To ... well, you get the idea. Most colleges and universities, as we said above, regard financial success as of ultimate value, and so they orient their degree programs toward that goal. Christian liberal arts colleges, on the other hand, regard students themselves as of ultimate value and so orient curricula toward students' flourishing. These approaches are obviously quite different. They're so different, in fact, that they employ entirely separate senses of value.

Certain things are valuable in themselves, while other things are valuable only instrumentally. Let me explain. To get the idea, consider a twenty-dollar bill. A twenty-dollar bill is valuable precisely because it can be traded up for something better (usually coffee, in my case). Twenty-dollar bills, in other words, have *instrumental* value. Now consider something, a human life or virtue, for example, whose value is had regardless of its relation to anything else. These have *intrinsic* value. Such things are valuable in themselves or in their own right, apart from their practical usefulness or anyone's opinion about them.

Christ-shaped liberal education structures its curriculum to focus on what is intrinsically valuable, because that is what is conducive for human flourishing. College education, on this view, is itself intrinsically valuable. On the alternative view, college is not really for *education*. Instead, it is recast as having merely instrumental value: college is for *professional training*. Now, let us be perfectly clear about this: the work we do at our jobs is both intrinsically valuable (because God created us to work) *and* instrumentally valuable (because it generates needed wealth). Let us also be clear that most jobs rightly require some sort of training. Still, the point remains: if college is only for the purpose of professional training, then college is simply an instrumental means to a job.

As persons created to flourish, we all have certain longings anchored deep within our souls, including the longings for meaning and purpose. It's not surprising, therefore, that bachelor's programs that inspire nothing beyond merely "meeting degree requirements" are frequently found unsatisfying. In his excellent book *The Purposeful Graduate,* Tim Clydesdale discusses the compelling findings of an eight-year, $225 million endeavor across eighty-eight campuses of higher education.[13] The endeavor, funded by the Lilly Endowment, studied the effect on undergraduate educational experience of intentionally engaging students on meaning and purpose. The results are unambiguous: *students thrive when their undergraduate education intentionally engages them on matters of purpose and meaning*. This is precisely what Christ-shaped liberal education does, ultimately grounding our meanings in God's creative intentions and our purposes in God's shalom.

CONSULTING THE ADVISORS: CONTOURS OF THE CURRICULUM

It will be apparent by now that Christ-shaped liberal education is focused less on churning out "experts" in this or that subject and more on realizing intrinsically good change within students through intellectual discipleship. The following chapters describe the main "arts" which together form the contours of Christian liberal arts education. Although the word "arts" typically is used to refer to the *fine arts* (painting or sculpture, for example), that is not its meaning in "liberal arts." The English term "liberal arts" traces to the Latin *artes liberales*. The Latin term *ars/artes* refers to some skill or practice (the skill of riding a horse well, for example). In this context we're interested in those skills or practices requisite for human flourishing, along with the knowledge appropriate to developing those skills.

The coming chapters focus on one *ars* apiece, and each explains how that skill connects to Christ-shaped liberal education. This little book does not discuss every liberal art. But I trust it says enough to help you along the journey toward Christian liberal arts education.

[1] J. R. R. Tolkien, "Letter to Geoffrey Smith (12 August 1916)," in *The Letters of J. R. R. Tolkien*, ed. Humphrey Carpenter (Boston: Houghton Mifflin, 1981), 10.

[2] Augustine, *City of God* 19.14, 14.28. Also, Augustine, *Confessions* 13.43.

[3] Cornelius Plantinga, Jr., *Not the Way It's Supposed to Be: A Breviary of Sin* (Grand Rapids, MI: Eerdmans, 1995), 10.

[4] These effects are further discussed in Paul. M. Gould, *The Outrageous Idea of the Missional Professor* (Eugene, OR: Wipf & Stock, 2014), 19-20.

[5] C. S. Lewis, *Mere Christianity* (New York: HarperOne, 1952), 71-72.

[6] Aristotle, *Nicomachean Ethics* books 1 and 2.

[7] Michael W. Austin, *Humility and Human Flourishing: A Study in Analytic Moral Theology* (New York: Oxford University Press, 2018), 16.

[8] C. S. Lewis, *The Problem of Pain* (New York: MacMillan, 1962), 53.

[9] Nicholas Wolterstorff, "Teaching for Shalom: On the Goal of Christian Collegiate Education," in *Educating for Shalom: Essays on Christian Education*, eds. Clarence W. Joldersma and Gloria Goris Stronks (Grand Rapids, MI: Eerdmans, 2004), 11.

[10] Martin Luther, "To the Christian Nobility," trans. Charles M. Jacobs, in *Luther: Selected Political Writings*, ed. J. M. Porter (Eugene, OR: Wipf and Stock, 2003), 42. This important point is discussed also in Tim Keller, *Every Good Endeavor: Connecting Your Work to God's Work* (New York: Penguin, 2012), 31-41.

[11] This is considered more deeply in R. Keith Loftin and Trey Dimsdale, eds., *Work: Theological Foundations and Practical Implications* (London: SCM Press, 2018).

[12] Robert George, "What's So Liberal about the Liberal Arts?" in *Liberal Democracy and Liberal Education*, ed. Daniel E. Cullen (New York: Lexington Books, 2017), 140.

[13] Tim Clydesdale, *The Purposeful Graduate* (Chicago: The University of Chicago Press, 2015).

2

PHILOSOPHY AND BRUSHING UP AGAINST ETERNAL TRUTHS

Travis Dickinson

PEOPLE HAVE QUESTIONED THE VALUE OF studying philosophy for a very long time. The playwright Aristophanes once mercilessly mocked Socrates, perhaps the most famous philosopher of all time, in his play *The Clouds* (423 BC). In the play Aristophanes makes Socrates headmaster of a school sarcastically named "The Thinkery" where students attempt to determine silly things like the distance a flea jumps and what causes the sound of a gnat. The speculation regarding the gnat, incidentally, is that the noise is caused by something of a trumpet in its backside. Aristophanes's point in the play is that doing philosophy is a colossal waste of time.

Today, the general attitude towards philosophy hasn't changed a whole lot. To be fair, there's not a direct line from studying philosophy to any specific career. Work in freelance philosophy today just is not what it once was! Still, those who demean philosophy seem to assume it should have some specific practical utility—and, according to some, measuring flea jumps is more practical than any outcome gained by studying philosophy.

My purpose in this chapter is to say why this view of philosophy is wrong. Though it may not have the specific practical utility some seek, philosophy possesses a variety of important values and, as we shall see, plays a crucial role in a Christ-shaped liberal education.

WHAT IS PHILOSOPHY?

So just what is philosophy? The term itself comes from two underlying Greek words that literally mean the love (*philo*) of wisdom (*sophia*). Many philosophers are no doubt lovers of wisdom, but the etymology doesn't convey much of what philosophy is. Philosophy may be more helpfully defined as thinking, with a careful use of logic, about fundamental and ultimate questions where the answers to these questions are taken for granted in our everyday pursuits. That's a mouthful, so let me explain.

Thinking carefully and logically. At the heart of philosophy is thinking carefully and making arguments that follow strict rules of logic. Of course, every academic discipline, when done properly, uses careful thought and makes logical arguments. However, given the abstract nature of the topics philosophy addresses, the case for a particular view will typically depend almost entirely on its arguments. With any issue, a philosopher wants to get really clear about the language and concepts, and then only proceeds in an argument when there are clear logical rules for making an inference.

Fundamental and ultimate questions. It is not easy to say what makes something fundamental or ultimate, but this feature gives philosophical questions their unique texture. Again, philosophical issues are typically abstract in that they are non-empirical. A question is non-empirical when the answer cannot be discovered through our five senses or things like the scientific method or experiments. Is Johnny in his room? The answer to this is an empirical matter and, as such, is not a philosophical issue. One simply needs to go check Johnny's room. What is the nature of being human? Well now, this is far more abstract and ultimate, and for that reason it is a philosophical issue. We cannot determine what a human is by any kind of lab experiment. This question will take careful, abstract reasoning and reflection (so it's abstract). And this question is, of course, fundamental in how we look at our fellow humans (so it's ultimate). Other quintessentially philosophical questions include: What makes an action morally right? What is the nature of truth? What is knowledge? What makes a society just? What qualifies as science? Does God exist?

Now, answers to philosophical questions, in virtue of being fundamental and ultimate, are typically *assumed in our everyday pursuits*. In a typical day, we likely go to work or school, we eat food, we may hang out with friends, watch a movie or read a book, build something, or help out a neighbor. As I discuss more fully below, there are a host of philosophical questions behind these sorts of pursuits. But philosophy is not done on the go, as it were. Philosophy is done, as it is sometimes said, in the armchair. Philosophy is a reflective discipline, deeply connected to how we live our lives.

GOODS OF THE MIND

If philosophy is thinking carefully about ultimate and fundamental questions, what good is engaging in philosophy when most people are content to assume answers? Why is philosophy not a colossal waste of time?

One great good of studying philosophy is developing the skills to think logically and critically. Bertrand Russell argued in an essay called "The Value of Philosophy" that many people miss philosophy's value because they are looking for the wrong thing.[1] It's easy to see the value of, say, science and technology because of all the things these disciplines give us. From science and tech we get iPhones, moon landings, gummy bears, modern transportation, air conditioning, cures for disease, and automated back scratchers. What does philosophy bring us? It obviously doesn't bring us material goods like these. But, Russell says, philosophy is not primarily aimed at providing material innovations. It is aimed rather at the "goods of the mind." The idea is that studying philosophy teaches us to think well. C. S. Lewis once remarked, "Good philosophy must exist, if for no other reason, because bad philosophy needs to be answered."[2] Lewis's point is that when we neglect philosophical reflection, or, as Lewis calls it, the "learned life," we can easily come under the influence of a bad philosophy. We need to study philosophy to gain the ability to critique and reject bad ideas, and that ability just is good philosophy.

Philosophy not only helps us to answer bad philosophical ideas, it also helps us to think well in all areas of life. In fact, philosophy helps one to think well even if some philosophical issue doesn't seem especially relevant to one's life. Studying that area of philosophy will teach one how to reason with careful logic and with the skills of critical thinking that may be applied to other areas of life.

To see this, consider an age-old philosophical controversy between Aristotelians and Platonists about the properties of a thing. The basic controversy is this: when you consider, say, three red things, do you have three different reds (Aristotelians) or one red instantiated in three different things (Platonism)? This is sometimes called the problem of the one and the many, and believe it or not this controversy has been alive and hopping for nearly twenty-four centuries! But this is a classic example of a controversy non-philosophers will struggle to care about. It seems like we are back to studying flea jumps here. Even if we grant for the moment that figuring out an answer to the problem of the one and the many will have little practical worth, studying this topic still has huge value. This is because if one studies the problem of the one and the many and comes to grasp the very subtle and nuanced ideas involved in this debate, one will have gained facility with the principles of logic and critical thinking. There's simply no other way to get into a philosophical issue like this. So, although a student may not have his or her life changed by studying the problem of the one and the many, he or she will certainly be changed by gaining the skills of logic and critical thinking which are then applicable to all other areas of life. And this is quite a value indeed.

Russell goes on to make the additional point that thinking well is almost always necessary for material innovations and inventions. How does the study of philosophy help innovation? Russell says it this way:

> the man who has no tincture of philosophy goes through life imprisoned in the prejudices derived from common sense, from the habitual beliefs of his age or his nation, and from convictions which have grown up in his mind without the co-operation or consent of his deliberate reason. To such a man the world tends to become definite, finite, obvious; common objects rouse no questions, and unfamiliar possibilities are contemptuously rejected.[3]

We live in a polarized world. People today seem locked into their views without the ability even to consider the possibility of an alternative view. But if a person is intellectually stuck in one narrow view of the world, then this person will be unlikely to discover any innovation when innovation is needed.

Russell says, "As soon as we begin to philosophize, on the contrary, we find that ... even the most everyday things lead to problems to which only very incomplete answers can be given."

None of us particularly likes incomplete answers, obviously, but incomplete answers can still have a powerful effect on us as knowers and ironically lead us to truth. Russell explains:

> Philosophy, though unable to tell us with certainty what is the true answer to the doubts which it raises, is able to suggest many possibilities which enlarge our thoughts and free them from the tyranny of custom. Thus, while diminishing our feeling of certainty as to what things are, it greatly increases our knowledge as to what they may be ... it keeps alive our sense of wonder by showing familiar things in an unfamiliar aspect.[4]

Once our thoughts are enlarged and freed, we are able to consider other possibilities which may turn out to be true and make a way for innovation.

IDEAS HAVE CONSEQUENCES

The second reason philosophy is not a colossal waste of time is that our ideas have consequences. The reality is whenever we act, we make *a lot* of assumptions. That is, with every intentional action, there are ideas underlying those actions. The question is whether we have rationally considered those ideas or not. One problem with today's widespread neglect of philosophy is that many people are not even aware of their philosophical assumptions.

To illustrate this, imagine one evening you're at home reading in your favorite chair. Suddenly the lightbulb in your reading lamp flickers a few times and then shuts off. You go to the closet where you keep the extra lightbulbs, pull one out of its cardboard wrapping, and proceed to change the lightbulb. Voila! Issue solved.

At first glance there is not much happening philosophically here. You don't have to claim, "I think, therefore, I am" to get a lightbulb changed! All you need is some basic practical knowledge and a spare lightbulb, and you are good to go.

It's true that you don't have to *do* philosophy (i.e., developing theories of philosophical reflection) in order to change a lightbulb. You are, nevertheless, making ultimate and fundamental philosophical assumptions in changing a lightbulb. You are assuming, for example, that there's a real material world of lightbulbs, lamps, electricity, and closets. After all, it's possible you are hallucinating (or having a vivid dream, or being manipulated in a computer-generated world or matrix) about having this experience. I realize this sounds farfetched and can even be difficult to take seriously, but I promise we are not measuring flea jumps in raising this! But no (sane) philosopher thinks it is actually the case that one is literally hallucinating, dreaming, or inhabiting *The Matrix* when they raise these thought experiments. Each of these is so farfetched that I think they are obviously false. But they are all clearly possible.

Consider the possibility of hallucination, for example. Isn't it at least possible (even if farfetched) that you are hallucinating the experience of reading this chapter right now? Here's why this is interesting: if you *were* hallucinating, and if nothing about the hallucination was out of the ordinary (i.e., the book didn't turn into a grizzly bear in a tutu playing the flute), how would you know that you were hallucinating? And so, if you are not hallucinating (which is what we all believe), how do you know that you're not? As it turns out, this is an interesting philosophical problem, and we assume an answer to it and a number of other philosophical questions when we change a lightbulb.

In the case of the lightbulb, things will likely work out just fine if you just change the lightbulb without considering the underlying philosophical ideas. But in other cases, we neglect the philosophical ideas to our great detriment and the detriment of others around us.

We don't have to look far for examples of philosophical ideas of significant consequence. Imagine Mrs. Smith is an elementary school teacher. Let's say Mrs. Smith is about to teach a history lesson to elementary aged students. Similar to the lightbulb example above, one assumes fundamental and ultimate questions in teaching any lesson. Mrs. Smith assumes things about the nature and purpose(s) of teaching. There will be a way she delivers the content of the lesson, a way she arranges the room. She may or may not allow the students to speak during the lesson, she may herself stand or sit, or she may integrate music or movement into the lesson. All of these things assume in different ways a philosophy of education. Again, Mrs. Smith has a philosophy of education whether she has reflected carefully about these matters or not. Obviously this really matters, since how a teacher approaches the teaching process impacts our most precious commodity—our kids!

This same insight extends to all other disciplines. A scientist assumes a philosophy of science when theorizing about the world. A businessperson assumes a philosophy of economics and a philosophy of work whenever he or she practices his or her business. Politicians have a political philosophy, lawyers and judges assume a philosophy of law, parents assume a philosophy of parental obligation, and pastors have a philosophy of ministry. The point is that there are, in every discipline (or career or ministry), important philosophical questions that should be addressed. To neglect these philosophical questions has a big impact on important parts of our lives.

As you develop a philosophical mindset, it becomes easy to recognize that philosophical ideas have consequences. Another example is the moral dimension of human actions. Some of our actions fall within the category of being either morally right or wrong. There's just no getting around the fact that determining whether an action is morally right takes philosophical reflection. Consider, for example, whether abortion is morally permissible. This is a weighty issue that—at least potentially—involves the destruction of a human life. How will you determine whether abortion is morally permissible? To have an informed view on this issue, you are going to have to think carefully about ultimate and fundamental questions regarding what a human person is and whether the unborn are human persons. This, as it turns out, is a philosophical issue with life or death consequences.

However, many of our actions are not straightforwardly moral. For example, deciding whether to brush your teeth in the morning does not seem to require a consideration of rightness or wrongness. If one forgets to brush, one has not done something morally wrong. But mundane tasks like teeth brushing do seem to have moral significance for living a virtuous life. Taking care of our bodies (teeth included!) and our health is an issue of virtue rather than right and wrong. So is how we spend our time and money, what we aim at in our careers, how we are obligated to treat and care for family members, and what we should do with our leisure time. Once again, determining what is the virtuous life is the domain of philosophy, and neglecting this important area of reflection almost guarantees we fail to be virtuous.

THE VALUE OF PHILOSOPHY FOR A CHRIST-SHAPED LIBERAL EDUCATION

This brings us to the value of philosophy for Christ-shaped liberal education. I'd like to suggest philosophy is not only valuable in the ways suggested above, but it is also simply good in itself. In other words, philosophy makes us better humans just in virtue of doing it. The reason that philosophy is intrinsically good is, firstly, because humans are designed to know. That is, knowing the world around us is part of what it is to be human. Aristotle, in his opening line to the *Metaphysics*, put it this way: "all men by nature desire to know." Aristotle's point is that knowledge of the world around us can certainly be useful, but more fundamentally knowing is simply a human good. It is part of our nature to know.

This is also implied by the so-called "creation mandate" in Genesis 1:28. After creating Adam and Eve, God mandates that they "subdue" the earth. The idea is that we are to make use of the earth and its resources for good purposes. But to subdue the world, we have to investigate and unlock the mysteries of the world around us. This suggests that God designed human beings to discover and to know. It seems we are designed with a natural sense of curiosity and wonder and, as such, knowledge and discovery is an important part of human flourishing as we live out our design.

Thus, philosophy, as a knowledge pursuit, is intrinsically good because it seeks to know the world. But in philosophy we seek to know the world at its deepest and most ultimate level. As it is sometimes said, "philosophy carves reality at its joints." True, it's possible for us to become so encumbered with the day to day of school, work, and other tasks that our sense of curiosity and wonder becomes diminished. We all come into the world as kids intensely curious about how things work, which is why kids ask so many questions (many of which turn out to be deeply philosophical!) and so enjoy stories and discovery. Studying philosophy prepares us to fulfill this curiosity in deep and fundamental ways. In doing so we live out our human curiosity, and this is good no matter what results come.

We are now in a position to see how philosophy is essential to Christ-shaped liberal education. We've seen that philosophy leads to human flourishing; asking the big and ultimate questions of life, seeking to think well, and pursuing a deep knowledge of the world just is the point of a liberal arts education. We do not simply seek technical skill to one day get a great paycheck. Rather, we seek to become most fully human and to flourish according to what and who we are. Again, there are big philosophical issues related to what and who we are. Thus, philosophy is crucial to liberal arts education as one of its core disciplines, but it is also crucial to determining how best to flourish.

The Christian answer is that humans flourish best when they have peace with God in the power of the gospel and live lives modeled after Christ. Philosophy, in a Christ-shaped liberal education, can play an important role in pointing us to God. This is because philosophy points us to and can awaken within us a thirst for the eternal. Philosophy in a way draws our attention away from the immediate desires for pleasure and material goods that so often, in our contemporary culture, command our attention. Doing philosophy forces us to bump into the transcendent and the eternal. Remember, the content of philosophy is non-empirical and abstract. This means that when we consider philosophical theories, we are often thinking about theories that are *necessarily* true if they are true at all. For example, if humans have inherent dignity and rights, then it doesn't matter how many humans there are, what they look like or act like, the nation of their citizenship, or their intellectual capacities. Humans have dignity and worth necessarily—they have it no matter what! This is a transcendent and eternal truth that directs our thoughts beyond the physical, material world. These transcendent and eternal categories point to a world beyond—and it is here that we find God waiting for us. When we try to explain why there are transcendent and eternal truths, it is natural to see God as the best and perhaps only explanation. Thus, our focus on philosophy naturally leads us to turn our thoughts and affections to God. Perhaps no greater reason can be given to study philosophy in the context of a Christ-shaped liberal education than the fact that it can lead us to the transcendent, to the eternal, and to a greater knowledge of God.

I conclude with a powerful example of this in the history of Christianity: the life transformation of Augustine (354-430). Before becoming one of the most important Christian theologians in the history of the church, Augustine lived a life of promiscuity and material gain. One day, as a young man, he was reading a philosophical work by the Latin philosopher Cicero titled *Hortensius* (unfortunately now lost to us). The book had a profound effect on Augustine. In his own words, he says:

> That book changed my mental attitude, and changed the character of my prayers to Thyself, O Lord. It altered my wishes and my desires. Suddenly, every vain hope became worthless to me and I yearned with unbelievable ardor of heart for the immortality of wisdom. I began to rise up, so that I might return to Thee.... The love of wisdom bears the Greek name, philosophy, and it was with this love that that book [*Hortensius*] enkindled me.... Since at that time, as thou knowest, O Light of my heart, the words of [Scripture] were unknown to me, I was delighted with Cicero's exhortation, at least enough so that I was stimulated by it, and enkindled and inflamed to love, to seek, to obtain, to hold, and to embrace, not this or that sect, but wisdom itself, wherever it might be.[5]

Philosophy awakened in Augustine a desire for the transcendent and the eternal—what he calls the "immortality of wisdom"—and led him to give up the fleeting pursuits of pleasure and vain desires. What's really interesting in Augustine's testimony, though, is how this yearning drew him to God. As Augustine says, "I began to rise up, so that I might return to Thee." A discovery of philosophy first set this great theologian on a trajectory towards the knowledge of God. He saw philosophy as what enkindled and inflamed a deep desire to seek with all of his heart the eternal wisdom "wherever it might be." And this eternal wisdom was ultimately found in the Christian gospel.

1 Bertrand Russell, *The Problems of Philosophy* (New York: Oxford University Press, 2001), 89ff.

2 C. S. Lewis, "Learning in War-Time," in *The Weight of Glory and Other Addresses* (Orlando, FL: Macmillan, 1980, rev. and exp. ed.), 28.

3 Russell, 91.

4 Russell, 91.

5 *Confessions* 3.4.7.

3

CONVERSING
WITH MASTERS

Humanities and the Great Books

Stephen D. Mizell

These books—or any such representative selection—speak most powerfully of what a human being can be. They dramatize the utmost any of us is capable of in love, suffering, and knowledge. They offer the most direct representation of the possibilities of civil existence and the disaster of its dissolution.[1]

AT THE END OF C. S. LEWIS'S *THE LAST BATTLE*,

Peter, Edmund, and Lucy are in awe that they've returned to Narnia. Aslan, you recall, had told them they couldn't return; yet, there they were. But Narnia seemed different. It seemed somehow more *vivid* than they remembered. Professor Digory Kirke explains to the children that they now have entered the *real* Narnia. The former Narnia was but a shadowland, and it was to the shadowland that Aslan forbid them to return. After his explanation Kirke adds under his breath, "It's all in Plato, all in Plato: bless me, what *do* they teach them at these schools?"[2]

If you're familiar with Plato, then you know that Kirke is referring to perhaps the most famous passage in all of Plato's writings: the allegory of the cave. That passage illustrates Plato's vision of reality as divided into two realms. The allegory begins with a description of a cave-like realm in which we confusedly perceive fleeting, ever-changing shadows. But beyond the mouth of the cave is another realm, fully sunlit, where dwell all things fully real and permanent—the realm where we experience what is true, good, and beautiful.[3] Peter, Edmund, and Lucy apparently hadn't learned Plato's allegory, for if they had, they would've easily understood Aslan's charge. What frustrates Kirke, and what his question implies, is that Plato isn't being taught in school. And why should that be so frustrating? Because, we can all but hear Kirke saying, Plato *should* be taught in school.

The assumption behind Kirke's question suggests a line of thinking that I want to develop. Students indeed *should* be taught Plato. Don't misunderstand this thought, though. I do not mean that students merely need to know *about* Plato. Students don't need merely a biographical sketch or summary of his philosophy. They don't need Plato trivia. They need Plato himself—and what's more, they need what he represents. Let me explain.

It's intriguing that Professor Kirke links Plato's allegory of the cave to the question of the children's education because the passage containing that allegory occurs in the middle of a lengthy discussion about education. Plato uses the allegory to illustrate something important about education. Education is not giving information to those who lack it. Education, he says, is not like putting sight into blind eyes. Instead, education "takes for granted that sight is there but that it isn't turned the right way or looking where it ought to look, and it tries to redirect it appropriately."[4] In other words, education—true education—does something to students. In saying that students need Plato, I'm saying they need the kind of education Plato describes. Education aligns (or perhaps re-aligns) students in a way that's appropriate to human beings—that is, appropriate to being *properly* human. Recognizing this need, the Roman philosopher Cicero, writing three centuries after Plato, described such an education as education *for humanity* or an education in the humanities.

But there's more. Students also need what Plato represents. You see, Plato embodies our need to converse about human experiences; and not just any experiences, but those that are universal for all humans across times and cultures. Such experiences are so important that people are often drawn to write books about them. Plato certainly did. Yet those who have read Plato's books know that there's no one quite like him. There is no substitute for reading *his* books. They stand out from the norm. They're powerful. And they're remembered. Plato's books are *great* books. His books are representative of all books that attain the status of greatness. So, in saying that students need what Plato represents, I'm suggesting that students need great books.

Students need great books in order to be educated to flourish as humans. This assumes something significant about how we understand a humanities education and, indeed, Christ-shaped liberal education. A humanities education may involve many things, but if it is truly an education for humanity, a humanities education must include in its focus the study of the great books. To see why this is so, we will need to look at, first, what are great books; second, what their role is in a humanities education; and finally, why you should be excited about studying them. As we proceed, I hope you will begin to see how a true humanities education—that is, an education for humanity informed by the study of the great books—is indistinguishable from Christ-shaped liberal education.

WHAT ARE THE GREAT BOOKS?

Students sometimes ask, what are the "great books"? The great books are a canon of books in the Western tradition that are the best which have been written. It might help to begin by pointing out what this *doesn't* mean. First, we're not talking about a fixed list of books. The canon of great books is open, meaning that any book has the potential to join this list. If a book meets certain criteria for being great, then it is a great book. Moreover, saying that a book is among the best to have been written doesn't mean that it embodies truth. Great books *converse* among themselves about the human condition. Conversations involve more than one party, and it's possible that at least one of those parties is mistaken. The Bible is the only great book we can assume to be true. We must evaluate the truth of other great books.

What are the distinguishing features of a *great* book? Roughly 130 million books have been written in human history. Why are so few of them considered great books, and who decides? These are not easy questions. First, it was long assumed that the great books were a collection of books that any educated person would know. Distinguishing the great books from the mass of published writings, therefore, was as simple as consulting someone with an education. Today, unfortunately, many leading universities don't expect students to read and know any list of books.

Second, descriptions of what makes a book great vary. This does not imply, however, that descriptions of greatness are merely expressions of preference. While different descriptions may reflect what different authors consider primary or more obvious characteristics of greatness, it is doubtful that these authors would see others' descriptions of greatness as entirely wide of the mark. What these varying descriptions indicate, in fact, is that greatness is a complex, finely textured concept that's difficult to encapsulate. We might compare this situation to that of car enthusiasts who, when asked what makes a car great, offer different descriptions. Each of them may emphasize certain characteristics over others, but most likely none would see other descriptions of what makes some cars great as altogether wrong. In short, there is general agreement on what characteristics are essential to greatness even though it may be difficult to express sufficiently all that greatness is.

The following four generally accepted criteria will give some idea of what sets apart a book as great.[5] One criterion is *endurance.* A great book deals with issues, problems, or facets of human life that transcend time, place, and culture. Countless books speak to the universal human condition, but the ideas of great books have stood the test of time. They've been read, analyzed, and remain relevant. Often, they acquire new significance even after the conditions that gave rise to them have faded. For example, though Blaise Pascal knew nothing of streaming video and ever-present social media, his musings on distractions seem pertinent when considering how we might use those technologies without becoming enslaved to them.[6]

Influence also sets apart a book as great. Influence refers partly to the great book's effect on culture, usually as part of its educational curricula. More significant, though, is how the book has contributed to the 'Great Conversation' about the human condition. A great book not only has something significant to say about the human condition; it also listens to what other great books say and notably modifies the trajectory of the conversation. A classic example is John Locke's *Second Treatise of Government.* Locke's concept of political authority based on God-given natural rights, which was influential in the birth of the U.S. Constitution, develops ideas of natural law found in Thomas

Aquinas' *Summa Theologiae*.[7] The contributions of great books to the ongoing Great Conversation about the human condition vary in *kind*, depending on whether they are works of philosophy, literature, or natural science, for example. Regardless of kind, however, great books share the trait of significance: what they say *matters*. Their contributions matter in a way that most books do not. Their contributions are integral to the Great Conversation and therefore shouldn't be ignored.

Great books are also *accessible*. Although copies of most great books are easy to obtain, that's not the sort of accessibility I have in mind here. Rather, what I mean is that the book is within the grasp of the average literate person. You don't need a PhD to read a great book. Perhaps C. S. Lewis best expresses this sense of accessibility when he writes:

> There is a strange idea abroad that in every subject the ancient books should be read only by professionals, and that the amateur should content himself with the modern books. Thus I have found as a tutor in English Literature that if the average student wants to find out something about Platonism, the very last thing he thinks of doing is to take a translation of Plato off the library shelf and read the *Symposium*…. If he only knew, the great man, just because of his greatness, is much more intelligible than his modern commentator. The simplest student will be able to understand, if not all, yet a very great deal of what Plato said; but hardly anyone can understand some modern books on Platonism.[8]

Of course, this doesn't mean that every great book is an easy read. Some are more difficult than others. Yet every year I teach students who initially assume the great books are beyond them, yet who happily discover that with a bit of guidance they can read these works with benefit and enjoyment. Despite the complexity and profundity of their topics, great books are eminently understandable.

Finally, great books are characterized by *excellence*. Great books are the best of their kind in terms of their form and content. What they express, they express well. Great books are the standard by which other books are measured. For example, Shakespeare's tragedies stand as exemplars for all tragedy. Great books combine richness and density in ways that are memorable. The oft-quoted beginning of Augustine's *Confessions* ("our heart is restless until it rests in you") strikes us as deeply meaningful and isn't easily dislodged from our minds.[9] Great books grip us. We might find that Alexis de Tocqueville moves us to defend liberty, for example, when we read, "I would, I think, have loved liberty in any age; but I feel inclined to worship it in the age in which we find ourselves."[10] In short, as the art of Michelangelo and Raphael outshine the work of all imitators, so the excellence of great books outshines all other works.

Now that we know what great books are and have a sense of what distinguishes them from all other books, let's turn our attention to their role in a humanities education.

EDUCATION FOR *HUMANITAS*: GREAT BOOKS AS MODELS OF VIRTUE

We noted at the beginning of this chapter that Cicero (following Plato) defines true education as education for *humanitas*. Such education is less concerned with what passes as humanities in many colleges and universities—namely, cultural studies or attempts to communicate experience through language. Instead, an education for *humanitas* is primarily concerned with helping students learn to flourish as human persons and citizens. Ideally, such an education would include every province of human knowledge. There is a sense in which a humanities education prepares students for every conceivable human enterprise. But don't misunderstand. A humanities education doesn't focus on teaching students literally every field, every job, every circumstance that touches human life. That's an impossible task, and a humanities education is more sensible than that. Instead, a humanities education cultivates students in the liberal arts—that is, those arts that are *appropriate* for humans as humans. As we have seen (chapter 1), the liberal arts refer less to a group of disciplines and more to the skills and knowledge that students need to be proper and good humans. This realization highlights the intrinsic value of a humanities education. It shifts the question from "What can I do *with* a humanities education?" to the more apt "What will a humanities education do *to* me?"[11]

Which skills, then, are appropriate to flourishing as human persons and citizens? To answer this, we must first answer the question, what is a human being? In answering this question, it becomes more evident that an education for *humanitas*, a Christian liberal arts education, and Christ-shaped liberal education all point to the same thing. Humans are rational beings made to be in fellowship with God and with each other. That is to say, we're made to live in harmony with our fellow man and God. In this, as Augustine observes, we love God in whom we find the proper way to love ourselves, which results in an obligation to love our neighbor by helping to improve his condition.[12]

We aren't born with a complete comprehension of human nature. We don't know ourselves, and because of that, we come into this world in many ways ignorant of what we are and how we should act. Moreover, sin has disrupted us. This is why we need an education for *humanitas*. A humanities education acquaints us with ourselves. It shows us that we *must* know ourselves. Socrates was correct when he said, "The unexamined life is not worth living for men."[13] But this acquainting with ourselves is not merely theoretical. An education for *humanitas* demands virtuous behavior, and virtue, as Cicero notes, "can best be summed up as right reason."[14] In saying this, we observe the connection between thinking and acting. "Right reason" refers to those intellectual and moral habits consistent with our nature. A humanities education—indeed, Christ-shaped liberal education—focuses on acquainting us with these habits of virtue so that we can be in harmony with God and one another.

Setting aside the obvious problem of sin misdirecting us from our God-ordained purpose, we cannot expect to develop habits of virtue accidentally. We acquire habits of virtue intentionally after much practice in consistently doing the right thing. Consistency, as any athlete knows, is essential. Without consistently performing the correct technique in practice, athletes cannot expect to perform well when it's game time. The problem is this: if we're ignorant about human nature before we begin attempting to form habits of virtue, then we can't be sure that we're doing the things that will result in habits of virtue. Our ignorance hamstrings us. If we wish to acquire the right habits, we need teachers, models of virtue who can instruct us in what it means to be properly human.

The role of such teacher-models in liberal arts education has been recognized since its beginning. In describing Socrates's role as a teacher, for example, Plato uses the rich metaphors of a midwife and a sower of seed.[15] For many, unfortunately, wise teachers who model virtue are rarely available. Much more accessible are books. Books allow for the dissemination of ideas, overcoming barriers of time and space. More importantly, books also tend to preserve the best of their author's thought. This is why, beginning in the Renaissance, an education for *humanitas* has treated books, particularly the great books, as the very best teachers available to students. As Lisa Richmond points out, an education in the great books is a listening in on the conversation of the best teachers in history and can even be a participation in that conversation.[16] As students listen in, the great books model for them the various habits of virtue appropriate for human beings. Participating in that conversation in any meaningful way demands that students practice the various habits of virtue modeled before them.

None of this diminishes the important role of teachers in learning communities. Christ-shaped liberal education readily esteems the teacher's vital role in students' development and ideally, listening to and participating in the great books' conversation takes place within a learning community. Education for *humanitas* entrusts the teacher of the Christian liberal arts with stewarding the tradition. The teacher is a guardian of a canon preserving the wisest teachers of all. He or she serves as an experienced guide for newcomers, helping them engage with the wisest teachers who model the habits of virtue needed for human flourishing.

DOORS OF OPPORTUNITY

Having the great books as your teachers is an exciting prospect. For one thing, you're studying with the *best* human teachers available. The great books offer thoughtful analyses of concepts, prudent solutions to problems, striking observations about the world, and depictions of beauty that move us. Even when they err, what they say is more thought-provoking than other books you will read, most other opinions you will hear, and definitely most of the pontifications of a faddish talking head on your phone or tablet. You cannot find better teachers than the great books.

Another reason for excitement is that studying the great books helps to reintegrate you. Christian students coming to college often are unaware of how fragmented their lives really are. They compartmentalize their private and public selves, disconnect their careers from their leisure, and falsely divide their lives into "sacred" and "secular" categories. Studying the great books not only reveals, but indeed rescues students from this fragmented state. The great books model the best practices for approaching the problems and issues of life as *whole* persons. When you read the great books, you quickly realize that their conversation isn't confined to specific fields of knowledge. Theology, philosophy, literature, history, and natural science all converse with one another because the subject of the conversation is the same: the human condition. In this, the great books help us see the *unity* of truth and work towards unifying us and our view of life. When this happens, you may find yourself being intentionally thoughtful about how each facet of your life fits into a harmonious picture. At that point, you've taken an important step toward living a life of integrity.

I've saved for last what's arguably the most exciting prospect education for *humanitas* offers: help finding your calling or vocation. Maybe you have an idea of what course of study you want to pursue because you've decided what kind of job you want. Maybe you've selected a course of study, but have no idea what you want to do when you receive your degree. Maybe you want to go to college, but don't know what to study and haven't given serious thought to what you'll do if you finish. No matter which of these situations applies to you, my recommendation is the same: pursue a humanities education that studies the great books. As you begin to understand yourself as a human and acquire the habits of virtue, you may find the great books awakening you. You may find yourself motivated to pursue careers you hadn't considered. More importantly, you may come to see your career as a way to improve the situation of your neighbor in some meaningful and productive way. When this happens, you've found your vocation.

CONCLUSION

Let me reiterate the central point of this chapter. Christ-shaped liberal education—a true humanities education—has as its focus the study of the great books. A Christian liberal arts education aims to develop those skills students need to fulfill their purpose as human beings. Careful engagement and interaction with the great books can be enormously helpful in acquiring those skills. Why? Because the great books are the best teachers. They model for us the habits of virtue we need to flourish. This constitutes the *essence* of a humanities education—that is, what's common among all the different academic disciplines within a Christian liberal arts education. That essence, that commonality, is the great books modeling habits of virtue and cultivating that same virtue in us as we listen and participate in their conversation.

The individual academic disciplines of Christian liberal arts education emphasize certain habits of virtue over others, which means that they'll pay more attention to those great books that most reflect those habits. Historians may highlight Thucydides and Herodotus. Philosophers have a special place for Plato and Aristotle. English teachers treasure Chaucer, Austen, and Whitman. For theologians, Augustine and Aquinas are respected. But in each case, it's the conversation of the great books that sets the standard of the humanities and Christ-shaped liberal education. The habits of virtue they set before us are the very liberal arts to which their namesake disciplines are devoted. The great books are the master teachers. A humanities education invites you to converse with the masters, guided by teachers to help you navigate your journey from the shadowland to the land of flourishing. And as Lewis once asked, "What could be better or more enjoyable than reading the greatest masterpieces of all time, under a man who has made them part of himself?"[17]

---

[1] Daniel Denby, *Great Books*, 2nd ed. (New York: Simon and Schuster, 2005), 461.

[2] C. S. Lewis, *The Last Battle* (New York: HarperTrophy, 1984), 212.

[3] See Plato, *Republic* 514a-18b.

[4] Ibid., 518d.

[5] What follows is a slightly modified version of Leland Ryken, *A Christian Guide to the Classics* (Wheaton: Crossway, 2015), 20-22. Note that what Ryken calls a "classic" I am calling a "great book."

[6] See Blaise Pascal, *Pensées*, 136.

[7] See John Locke, *Second Treatise of Government*, ed. C. B. Macpherson (Indianapolis: Hackett, 1980), chs. 2-5; Thomas Aquinas, *Summa Theologiae* I-II, q. 90, 92, 94-95.

[8] C. S. Lewis, "On the Reading of Old Books," in *God in the Dock: Essays on Theology and Ethics*, ed. Walter Hooper (Grand Rapids: Eerdmans, 1979), 217-18.

[9] Augustine, *Confessions* 1.1.

[10] Alexis de Tocqueville, *Democracy in America*, trans. Stephen D. Grant (Indianapolis: Hackett, 2000), 309.

[11] Arthur F. Holmes makes s similar point in *The Idea of a Christian College*, rev. ed. (Grand Rapids: Eerdmans, 1987), 24.

[12] Augustine, *City of God* 19.14.

[13] Plato, *Apology* 38a.

[14] Cicero, *Tusculan Disputations* 4.34.

[15] See Plato, *Theaetetus* 149a-51d and *Phaedrus* 276b-77a.

[16] Lisa Richmond, "Liberal Education and Book Learning," in *Liberal Arts for the Christian Life*, ed. Jeffry C. Davis and Philip G. Ryken (Wheaton: Crossway, 2012), 51.

[17] C. S. Lewis, letter to his father, February 16, 1914.

4

BIBLICAL STUDIES AND CHRISTIAN LIBERAL ARTS EDUCATION

David Lyle Jeffrey and R. Keith Loftin

IT'S HARDLY BREAKING NEWS THAT THE BIBLE holds an important place in the Christian life. Christian believers in the eternal, all-knowing, all-powerful creator of the universe rightly prize the Bible as *God's* word. Yet, while many Christians have no difficulty seeing the Bible's importance for worship and their devotional lives, when it comes to thinking of the Bible as an integral part of college education things are less clear. Church attendance and one's private spiritual growth, after all, are familiar as *sacred*. But unless you're studying to become a pastor, you might think college education is *secular*. It's not really anti-sacred, but it's just not a place one expects to find the Bible, right?

This echoes a question posed in the early 300s by the Christian writer Tertullian: "what has Athens to do with Jerusalem?"[1] Or for our context, what has college education to do with the

Bible? We want to argue in this chapter that, actually, students—especially Christian students—have convincing reasons to seek out an undergraduate education that includes biblical studies. By "includes" we don't mean ordinary degree programs plus a Bible class or two sprinkled on top; our claim is that the truest and highest goals of education demand a curriculum that truly *integrates* the Bible throughout. Since this approach is characteristic of Christ-shaped liberal education, students ought to give serious consideration to enrolling in a Christian liberal arts college.

THE BIBLE AMONG CULTURAL AUTHORITIES

Contemporary culture is sharply at odds with biblical thinking. Biblical values are regularly disparaged in the public square, and biblically informed education is increasingly marginalized.[2] In fact, our contemporaries find the Bible *offensive*. It's not just that the Bible is counter-cultural, although that is true. The issue is that the intrinsic character of the Bible, namely its claim to be the word of God, contradicts the presuppositions of modern, secular college education.

Consider the Bible's claim: there is a God, and he cares about the way we live. In the Bible this claim is not offered on the grounds of superior philosophical argument, rhetorical persuasion, or political power. The Bible presents a comprehensive series of moral claims advanced not on the basis of intellectual deliberation or political process, but rather as a direct self-disclosure of God. The Bible reveals God as *personal*. As personal, God speaks and gives instructions to his people (through Moses and other prophets, for example). God reveals himself as one who relates to human persons.

What stands out about the connection between the Bible's moral claims and the way God is revealed is that, unlike us, God is *holy*. God is singularly perfect, and this is the defining fact underlying how God relates to his creation. God's specific instructions for life in this world take the legal form of a covenant, with mutual obligations and optimal directions required for humans to flourish and *shalom* to be achieved. Not only is God (as the creator) in a good position to actually know what is required for humans to flourish, but as holy God bears *authority* over all of life.

It is the Bible's claim that God bears authority over all of life that contemporary culture finds offensive. Nothing could be more alien to modern and postmodern minds than such a claim. The entire history of modernity, as philosopher Hannah Arendt has famously argued, has been characterized by challenges to authority of every kind.[3] The authority of the Bible has often been first in the firing line. Its forthright and totalizing claims upon human behavior, for example, made the Bible's authority a primary casualty of the French Revolution. The Marxism and Nazism prominent in the 19th and 20th centuries targeted biblical authority because it was deemed entirely incompatible with another authority then bidding for supremacy, namely the absolute authority of government. Similar examples abound, but here's the point: claiming that God himself has laid moral obligations upon our lives is infuriating to our contemporaries who wish to advance a contrary vision of how we ought to live.

Needless to say, if God truly exists, then this makes a difference to how we are to live. It must be remembered that, along with revealing God's instructions for living, the Bible's moral teaching includes the inescapable reality that there are consequences for how we live. This moral order is a *given*—rather than a socially constructed—feature of the reality we inhabit. This idea that there's an actual divine law which God has given and still cares about is assumed and even cherished historically. This is evident in Roman history, for instance, from the fourth century emperor Constantine to the eighth century emperor Charlemagne, as well as in the laws of English-speaking peoples from Henri de Bracton's *Laws of England* (1250s) to the *Institutes of the*

Laws of England of Edward Coke (1600s) and William Black-stone's *Commentaries on the Laws of England* (1760s).

This idea, unfortunately, has been largely rejected in our day. Why? Again, it's because contemporary culture will not tolerate the suggestion that there's a higher, universal source of authority by which our own authority may be judged. For this reason contemporary rejection of the Bible's authority makes sense, because those who reject the idea that there's a God to whom all are accountable naturally believe it is destructive to social wellbeing for those who uphold the Bible's authority to claim the opposite. This, in turn, makes it unsurprising that neither the purposes nor the curricula of modern secular education have much of a place for the Bible.

FLOURISHING AND THE BIBLICAL ETHOS

Recall from chapter one of this book that people flourish when they live the lives God intends for them, and that is the major focus of Christ-shaped liberal education. If *all* of life falls under God's authority, then this includes education. People of the book,[4] therefore, should be mindful of the reason(s) God provided revelation in the first place. To borrow from the argument of Steven Kepnes, a professor of Jewish studies at Colgate University, "The purpose of the Jewish law is precisely to map out a path through which the people [of] Israel can follow the commandment of God to be holy."[5] This is important because holiness just is God's prescription for human flourishing: "You must be holy because I, the LORD your God, am holy" (Lev. 19:2, NET). Keeping in mind the Bible's claim to authority, it's worth emphasizing that God reveals this as a *command* rather than a mere suggestion.

The Bible connects (e.g., Deuteronomy 32:2 and Psalm 1) our obeying God's commands—that is, holy living—and our flourishing against the backdrop of our being created in the image of

God (Genesis 1:26-27). In the image of the *holy* God, that is. Not only understanding but indeed *embodying* that reality in our lives is what holiness is about. When it comes to questions about how to achieve a flourishing life, the Bible's answer is not merely, "God said it," but rather, "God has revealed something profound about his own nature, namely that he is holy, and he wills our participation in his life." For our part, fulfilling God's call to such a life demands deep reflection on the patterns and purposes of how we live, along with sustained, continual practice. This is no doubt why the instructions found in Leviticus 19 are so detailed. As Kepnes explains, "That the ethical commandments are included along with the ritual commandments in a code of holiness means that there is a holy dimension to ethics and an ethical dimension to holiness."[6] This adds up to an ethos that is to inform not only our education but our lives comprehensively.

This biblical ethos fundamentally guides both the general approach to education as well as the specific course requirements of Christian liberal arts colleges. That is a defining characteristic of Christ-shaped liberal education. This doesn't mean the Bible is the (only) textbook for every class or that class lectures are all replaced with Bible studies. But it does mean that, inasmuch as education is concerned with flourishing and flourishing is inseparable from the biblical ethos, students seeking education *for life* have strong reasons to enroll in a Christian liberal arts college.

THE BIBLE AMONG THE GREAT BOOKS

Liberal arts education—especially its *humanities* component—initiates a student into what is often called "the Great Conversation." That is to say, students are prompted to regard themselves as entering, although haltingly, perhaps, into dialogue with the great texts which form the repository of Western civilization. Not only are these texts regarded as excellent examples of *how* to discuss the great ideas, they are also, as Robert Hutchins points out, "the means of understanding our society and ourselves. They contain the great ideas that dominate us without our knowing it."[7] The voices of the great books offer an uninterrupted, centuries-long conversation about the ideas and questions that, at their deepest level, define the human condition and point us toward the pathway to human flourishing.

Encountering and engaging in the Great Conversation changes a person. Studying the greatest books of Western civilization will shape a student's soul, and for this reason it has been prized in liberal arts education since the ancient world. The ancient Roman statesman Cicero (106-43 BC), for example, praised such study for its *humanizing* effect, that is, its ability to encourage us toward the life most befitting humans.[8] In a letter offering advice about how to think of education, the great Italian Renaissance scholar Leonardo Bruni (1370-1444) likened reading the great books to choosing which foods to eat: "just as those who care about their stomachs do not pour just any kind of food into them, so one who wants to preserve the integrity of his mind will not permit it just any reading whatsoever. We must endeavor, therefore, to read nothing but the best and most universally approved works."[9] The best conversationalists are indeed the most worthwhile to engage in conversation.

The same idea is present in the Christian liberal arts tradition. The church father Basil of Caesarea (330-379), one of the most important figures in Christian history, pressed his students to read the great books—those writings associated with "the learned men of old"—but to do so with care as Christians: "This is my counsel, that you should not unqualifiedly give your minds to these men, as a ship is surrendered to the rudder ... but that, while receiving whatever of value they have to offer, you yet recognize what it is wise to ignore."[10] Basil goes on to explain to his students that there is tremendous value to be found amongst the great books, so that even Christians should not shy from gleaning whatever truth, beauty, and goodness may be found there.

Christ-shaped liberal education, though, recognizes that these gleanings cannot fully satisfy the soul's desire to learn how to flourish. For this, one must move beyond the great books to the Greatest Book, namely, the Bible. "Into the life eternal," Basil continues, "the Holy Scriptures lead us, which teach us through divine words."[11] Just as a great admirer of Rembrandt's paintings would never prefer replicas to gazing upon the original *Storm on the Sea of Galilee,* so students who desire to flourish must seek an education that includes actually studying the Bible.

Allowing the biblical ethos to guide how we approach education and degree programs is, as we've seen, important. But it's not enough. Christian liberal arts education includes the study of the Bible itself. Why? Here are two reasons. First, it's the word of *God.* In studying the Bible we're entering into conversation with God himself—not simply one of the insightful "learned men of old" but indeed the omniscient Author of life himself. Second, if the issue most fundamental to human flourishing is man's relation to the creator, then our education must include studying the words written by the God who knows most intimately how we're supposed to function, what has gone wrong with us, and who has communicated how to live in a broken world.

THE BIBLE AND WESTERN HERITAGE

An important way of thinking about the Great Conversation, that centuries-long conversation discussed above, is in terms of a *dialogue.* But not just any dialogue; this dialogue, Hutchins says, is the defining hallmark of Western civilization. "The tradition of the West," he explains, "is embodied in the Great Conversation ... that continues to the present day. Whatever the merits of other civilizations in other respects, no civilization is like that of the West in this respect."[12] What does this mean? The idea is not that one studies the great books in order to discover what one is "supposed to" think as a member of Western civilization. Quite the contrary, in fact, for these books comprise a *dialogue*, and of course there would be little need for dialogue were everyone in agreement. Hutchins's point, rather, is that we are the inheritors of a civilization whose defining characteristic is its perpetual dialogue about the great ideas. Participation in this dialogue formed the headwaters that fed, historically, the various streams of what came to be called the liberal arts. It is well known that that dialogue, along with the various disciplines (arts) attendant to it, has molded Western societies and intellectual culture for centuries.

The full history of *how* that dialogue has molded Western civilization is both fascinating and instructive for our contemporary world (if you want to learn that story in full you'll have to enroll in a Christian liberal arts college!). At every step throughout that history, the influence of the Bible was critical. "Genetically speaking," David Lyle Jeffrey writes, the "development of the humanities disciplines in Western culture cannot be fully understood apart from an appreciation of scriptural husbandry and ... a kind of ecclesiastical mothering which, together, have birthed and nurtured Western intellectual life down to the present age."[13] In other words, the story of Western civilization's development is incomplete apart from the role of the Bible upon it. The shaping effect, throughout history, of the Bible's ideas on institutions and individual thinkers alike can scarcely be exaggerated. This effect is not limited to religious history or religious instruction. Indeed,

> classical learning, indeed all types of learning in the monasteries and other communities of Christian education, was organized around a *studium* [study] whose central preoccupation was with the Bible as a foundation for *all* learning. It was the study of the Bible ... far more than the study of Cicero and the classical authors generally that spread Latin literacy *and* produced also a textual tradition of several European

vernaculars.... [N]ot only was the Bible in such a fashion made foundational for general humane learning in European culture, but that without it, much of Roman secular learning and many of the ancient texts themselves would not have survived to be a part of our culture at all.[14]

The influence of the Bible lies at the very heart of both the institutions and the individual thinkers foundational to Western civilization's development. In studying the Bible, then, you are studying the text that is most influential in the development of Western societies and centers of culture.

Far from being a simple "add on" to college, the Bible is foundational to the most engaging and worthwhile education available—but available, in its truest form, only at Christian liberal arts colleges. Secular universities, after all, are offended by the Bible's claim to authority as the words of a holy God; their curricula preserve neither a place for nor the purposes of the Bible. Yet Christ-shaped liberal education takes seriously the ethos of the Bible, allowing it to guide its overall approach to education and even the specific course requirements of degree programs. As students encounter and are initiated into the Great Conversation, as they engage in that dialogue with the great books about the great ideas, they experience its *humanizing* effect of encouraging us toward the life most befitting humans (flourishing). Christian liberal arts colleges recognize, though, the necessity of moving beyond the great books to read also the Greatest Book—the words of the Author of life and flourishing himself. Students, therefore, in search of the most complete education ought to give serious consideration to enrolling in a Christian liberal arts college.

1 Tertullian, *Prescription Against Heretics* 7.19.

2 Some of the central reasons are ably addressed in *The Bible and the University*, eds. David Lyle Jeffrey and C. Stephen Evans (Grand Rapids, MI: Zondervan, 2007).

3 Hannah Arendt, *Between Past and Future* (New York: Penguin, 1968).

4 This phrase commonly refers to both adherents of Judaism and Christianity. See David Lyle Jeffrey, *People of the Book: Christian Identity and Literary Culture* (Grand Rapids, MI: Eerdmans, 1996) for discussion of how the Bible has shaped the identity and literary culture of Western Christians.

5 Steven Kepnes, *The Future of Jewish Theology* (Malden, MA: Wiley-Blackwell, 2013), 4.

6 Kepnes, *Future of Jewish Theology*, 104.

7 Robert M. Hutchins, *The Great Conversation: The Substance of a Liberal Education* (Chicago: Encyclopedia Britannica, 1952), 2.

8 Marcus Tullius Cicero, *De Oratore* 3.21-22, 58 and *Pro Archia* 2-4.

9 Quoted in Robert E. Proctor, *Defining the Humanities: How Rediscovering a Tradition Can Improve Our Schools*, 2d ed. (Bloomington: Indiana University Press, 1998), 5.

10 Basil of Caesarea, *Address to the Young Men on the Right Use of Greek Literature* 1.

11 Ibid., 2.

12 Hutchins, *The Great Conversation*, 1.

13 David Lyle Jeffrey, "Scripture in the *Studium* and the Rise of the Humanities," in *Re-envisioning Christian Humanism: Education and the Restoration of Humanity*, ed. Jens Zimmermann (New York: Oxford University Press, 2017), 164-165.

14 *The Bible and the University*, 7.

5

BETTER TOGETHER

Why Christians Need Literature and
Literature Needs Christians

Marybeth Baggett

SHIRLEY JACKSON'S "THE LOTTERY" BEGINS
harmlessly enough—with townspeople from a rural community
gathering in the picturesque public square on an idyllic June
day.[1] Schoolboys in their newfound summer freedom collect
rocks, neighbors chat while waiting for some sort of ceremony to
begin, and town officials make their final preparations for the
event. But this account of small-town camaraderie takes a dark
turn, as first the Hutchinson family is singled out after drawing
the fateful paper marked with an ominous black dot. Eventually,
Tessie, the Hutchinson mother, finds herself holding the dreaded
slip. Her earlier joking mood shifts to loud protests, challenging
the contest's outcome: "You didn't give him time enough to take

any paper he wanted. I saw you. It wasn't fair!" And as Tessie pleads for her daughter and son-in-law's inclusion in the second round of drawing paper slips from the dilapidated box, it dawns on the reader that this is not a lottery one wants to win, a realization confirmed once the rocks start flying.

When *The New Yorker* first published "The Lottery" in 1948, the reader reaction was overwhelming. People wrote demanding to know what it meant. Many were frustrated and outraged by the events depicted and appalled that the magazine would dare run such a piece. Miriam Friend's response captured the general bewilderment: without "a brief explanation" of the tale, she said, she and her husband would "scratch right through [their] scalps trying to fathom it."[2] And Carolyn Green wondered at the "shock and horror" Jackson's story provoked, yet even still she had the sense that there might be something of genius about it.[3] All told the magazine received over three hundred letters in response, well beyond anything they'd ever published.[4]

Anyone who has read Jackson's story can understand the commotion its publication raised. Jackson sets readers up to expect one outcome and delivers quite the opposite. The plot appears quite benign but is in fact alarming. A re-read, however, reveals Jackson's skillful crafting of the story with the clear intention to unsettle readers. Through her careful arrangement, she highlights how the town's surrender to the status quo, to groupthink, and to blind tradition leads them to such inhumanity and, importantly, that those same tendencies may (and probably do) also lurk in the reader's heart. The story's content, in other words, cannot be disentangled from its form, at least not without the loss of something valuable.

WHAT LITERATURE DOES

This is exactly the kind of thing any well-made story does. By involving the imagination, it gestures beyond the literal confines of the events described and captures the reader's heart as well as her mind. The same holds for a well-made poem. *Perrine's Literature*, a popular anthology, explains that poetry invites us to participate imaginatively in experience, by broadening it or deepening it. What the editors say of poetry is true of any solid literary work: it's a multi-dimensional form of language, appealing to the intellectual, sensual, emotional, and imaginative faculties of readers.[5]

A quick example nicely illustrates this operation. Wanting to learn about the eagle, you might review the *Encyclopedia Britannica* entry on the creature. There you'll learn that eagles are "large, heavy-beaked, big-footed birds of prey," that they belong to the Accipitridae family and are kin to falcons, buzzards, and other winged predators. The article is chock-full of facts, explaining that the eagle resembles a vulture in body composition and its flight patterns but differs by having a fully feathered head and "strong feet equipped with great curved talons." We learn, too, about the animal's foraging habits, its preference for live prey, and its reliance on strength and surprise over agility to dominate its quarry.[6]

It's not exactly a page-turner, nor was it meant to be. While a reference article can tell you about the eagle, literature can *show* you. It can invite you to experience the facts the encyclopedia lays out, to give them a full-bodied expression. Consider "The Eagle" by Alfred, Lord Tennyson:

> He clasps the crag with crooked hands;
> Close to the sun in lonely lands,
> Ring'd with the azure world, he stands.
>
> The wrinkled sea beneath him crawls;
> He watches from his mountain walls,
> And like a thunderbolt he falls.[7]

Through imagery, rhyme, and figurative speech, Tennyson brings the eagle to poetic life in the reader's mind. The difference between the reference article and Tennyson's poem exemplifies the different types of knowledge that C. S. Lewis discusses in "Meditation in a Toolshed."[8] Standing in a dark toolshed, Lewis noticed a sunbeam coming through a crack in the door. All around the beam was darkness, and in the beam he saw specks of dust floating. As he took a small step into the light, however, a whole new scene came into view. He could see the outside world with its leaves and trees and sun, obscured before from his perspective.

Lewis uses this experience as an allegory for "looking at" a phenomenon versus "looking along" it. The ecstatic, resplendent, consuming experience of love, for example, is a far cry from a biologist's factual explanation of its chemical processes. A Shakespearean sonnet is much closer to the former than the latter. In this way, excellent literature offers insights into the human condition unavailable from the sciences, or even philosophy, and it does so in memorably engaging ways that are themselves quite valuable. Literature both teaches and delights, as the Roman poet Horace famously put it.[9] Its inherent value has been recognized by thinkers through the ages, including by church fathers, many of whom found resonances between even great pagan literature, such as that of Homer and Hesiod, Aeschylus and Sophocles, and fundamental truths of scripture.

READING WIDELY

This might strike us as contradictory. If literature delivers knowledge, wouldn't Christians find value only in the writings of those who embrace the truth of the gospel? Poet Luci Shaw grounds her answer to this question in the Christian belief that all human beings are made in the image of God and have access to general revelation: "We who believe we bear God's image must realize that that image includes the capacity to imagine and create, because God is himself an imaginative Creator. Though we cannot produce something out of nothing, as God did, we can combine the elements and forms available to us in striking and original ways that arise out of the unique human ability (designed and built into us by God) to imagine, to see pictures in our heads."[10]

A precious product of the human imagination, literature—with all its distinctive tools at its disposal—can powerfully reveal both the potential and pitfall of the human condition, its beauty and ugliness, its virtue and vice, its hunger for wholeness and besetting brokenness. It instills within us both despair, on the one hand, and the yearning hope for redemption, on the other. It reminds us that we have been made in the very image of God, filled with transcendent longings and tastes for enchantment, and that we are fallen creatures, too often content to settle for less than we're meant for, exchanging our sacred birthright and noble calling for a bowl of porridge. It shows us at our best and our worst, revealing our convictions and compromises, our courage and cowardice, both the angels of our better nature and our inner haunting demons. It reveals both the extravagant goodness to which we're called and how far short of it we can fall, both the goodness to which we feel pulled, and the grace we desperately need.

Christians can and should study a range of literary texts, both sacred and secular, to glean wisdom from those who have gone before us. Basil of Caesarea wrote an address to Christians along these lines, encouraging the proper use of pagan literatures. He found freedom in Christianity for such study and even precedence among Old Testament figures like Moses and Daniel who had steeped themselves in their respective pagan cultures. For those secure in their convictions, especially, study of other literatures can further solidify those beliefs. Basil explained, "If, then, there is any affinity between the two literatures, a knowledge of them should be useful to us in our search for truth;

if not, the comparison, by emphasizing the contrast, will be of no small service in strengthening our regard for the better one."[11]

THE PLEASURE OF THE TEXT

In addition to wisdom, excellent literary works also offer delight. Lewis often points to the pleasure of reading when speaking of its value. In his ingenious *Screwtape Letters*, a satirical novel depicting a demon advising his nephew on temptation, the older demon, Screwtape, lays into his benighted protégé, Wormwood, who had made a grave mistake by allowing his "patient" to read a book and take a walk for no reason other than enjoyment. This sounds harmless enough, yet Screwtape realizes that this direct experience of genuine pleasure facilitated for the patient a "second conversion," a personal encounter with the source of that pleasure, namely God himself. It would have been better for the demons' purposes if the patient had read the book to impress others, to make witty remarks upon it, or otherwise to self-aggrandize. Instead, the patient's innate desire for the good was satisfied by an authentic delight of an intrinsically delightful book. This pleasurable experience, Screwtape realizes, has provided the patient with a "touchstone of reality" not easily dislodged by counterfeits. And the more the patient embraces that touchstone, the more intimately connected he is with God and, by extension, with himself.

The kind of enjoyment Screwtape fears, enjoyment of something worthwhile for its own sake and not for self-advantage, becomes simultaneously a pathway to God and a hedge against delusion. In Screwtape's words, his hostility notwithstanding, "The man who truly and disinterestedly enjoys any one thing in the world, for its own sake, and without caring twopence what other people say about it, is by that very fact fore-armed against some of our subtlest modes of attack."[12] What Screwtape unwittingly offers readers is thus a parable of spiritual awakening and discipleship, with the written word—most likely a story, given Lewis's literary background and creative work—as the catalyst.

In this way, *The Screwtape Letters* both promotes and exemplifies the value of literature to a Christian liberal arts education. As we've noted, the so-called patient is benefited by his exposure to the goodness of this enjoyable written word. It enables in him repentance and a renewal of grace, a kind of self-recovery and reunion with God. But on another level, Lewis's book itself exudes the good, the true, and the beautiful, inviting his readers to partake of the very same enchantment the fictional patient does. While Lewis's character may be made up, the scenario described tells us much about our reality; not to mention, with its imaginative twists, the book is wildly fun to read, and reread.

LITERARY TRUTH, GOODNESS, AND BEAUTY

Literature can give us ears to hear and sensitize our eyes to see goodness, truth, and beauty—in fact to effect union with God himself, as David Lyle Jeffrey and Gregory Maillet explain in *Christianity and Literature*: "The core of Christian theological aesthetics is the religious experience of reestablished communion with God, mediated in this case by aesthetic structures which create, facilitate or sometimes even require a triune meeting with the work of literary art, the spiritually awakened human person, and the divine life of God revealed by faith and reason."[13] In this way, literature—correctly understood—contributes to a life of human flourishing. Drawing on the doctrines of creation, the incarnation, and the resurrection, Susan Gallagher and Roger Lundin argue that the world in which we live is filled to the brim with meaning and purpose. The reading and writing of literature, they explain, can train us to discern that significance, a crucial element of our calling as stewards of that world. The reading and writing of literature, Gallagher and Lundin explain, "enables us to respond to the order, beauty, and grace of God and his world and to the disorder that our sin has brought into that world."[14]

A rudimentary form of this argument comes through Samuel Coleridge's *Biographia Literaria*, wherein the Romantic poet explores the role of the imagination and traces it back to its source in God. [15] For Coleridge, the imagination is the epitome of creativity, necessary for life and restoration of divisions or destruction in this fallen world. Only through the imagination can reconciliation take place, a process mirrored by poets as they harmonize the opposites one finds in this world, especially the universal and particular. In this way, Coleridge's theory of the imagination stems from his Christian beliefs wherein Christ is the ultimate reconciler, connecting and redeeming all. The human imagination, by echoing Christ's redemptive work, looks back to the unadulterated goodness of the created order and forward to God's consummation of history.

Throughout the creation story in Genesis, God affirms that the created order is good, a category that points to more than just the moral, as Robert Adams articulates in *Finite and Infinite Goods: A Framework for Ethics*.[16] Both the aesthetic and intellectual fit here too, and literature at its best is replete with these excellencies, available for students and other readers to discover and appreciate, relish and savor. 2 Peter 1 echoes this argument, explaining that God is the source of life, glory, and excellence and that these gifts allow us to partake in the divine nature, enabling for us our flourishing. James 1:17, too, tells us that "[e]very good gift and every perfect gift is from above" (ESV). On such grounds, Adams, as an ethicist, binds together desiring the excellent with the qualifications for living a moral life, arguing that the "good" for a person "is a life characterized by enjoyment of the excellent."[17] He argues further that a good person is one who is *for* the good.[18]

If we are to accept this understanding of goodness as deriving from God, discerning, desiring, and pursuing the excellent ultimately helps orient our minds toward God and enlarge our understanding of worship as daily practice, a mode of living and flourishing. Our everyday actions and our engagement with others should be bound up in this sacred undertaking: discerning, encouraging, and practicing the excellent, as a means to know, recognize, worship, and follow God. Indeed, arguably it's our *obligation* as Christians to do so. Gene Edward Veith explains, in *Reading between the Lines*, that "[t]he process of learning how to enjoy (subjectively) what is admirable (objectively) is known as the cultivation of tastes... What we delight in has a spiritual dimension."[19] As Philippians 4:8 phrases it: "Finally, brothers, whatever is true, whatever is honorable, whatever is just, whatever is pure, whatever is lovely, whatever is commendable, if there is any excellence, if there is anything worthy of praise, think about these things" (ESV). Adams goes as far as to say that "loving the excellent has the more foundational role" than even doing one's moral duty.[20]

OUR CONTEMPORARY MOMENT

Rightly construed, literature can draw us closer to union with God and with other people. There have been two extreme errors that literary study in the secular realm has been drawn to, both of which in different ways position man as the source of literary value. On one hand, there are those who are tempted to elevate the literary texts themselves. Recognizing the inherent value of literary art, they might mistake that value as an end in itself, thus ignoring (or downright denying) the foundation that undergirds and sustains it. Such is the case of Matthew Arnold and the program of literary studies he instituted at the end of the nineteenth century. As the Victorian era was coming to a close, Arnold recognized the need for a stabilizing force to counterbalance the social upheaval wrought by industrialization, Darwinism, and the rise of the middle class. Religion, Arnold believed, had failed, and with utopian naiveté, Arnold's project suggested that literary instruction alone might prove a worthy substitute to sustain a thriving culture.

On the other extreme, the literary field of today is dominated by ideological criticism rather than Arnold's pursuit of truth, goodness, and beauty, misguided as he was about the source of those objective values. In a bestselling handbook to literary theory, for example, Terry Eagleton scoffs at the notion that literature has any inherent value:

> There is no such thing as a literary work or tradition which is valuable in itself, regardless of what anyone might have said or come to say about it. "Value" is a transitive term: it means whatever is valued by certain people in specific situations, according to particular criteria and in the light of given purposes. It is thus quite possible that, given a deep enough transformation of our history, we may in the future produce a society which is unable to get anything at all out of Shakespeare. His works might simply seem desperately alien, full of styles of thought and feeling which such a society found limited or irrelevant.[21]

Here of course Eagleton is blurring the lines between the objective fact of value and the personal (or even collective) act of valuing something. By doing so, he discards the possibility that someone or some society might be wrong in their valuation. Even *the mere idea* of a wrong evaluation or a wrong assessment makes no sense on Eagleton's account. This sets the field of literary study up to be little more than power struggles. If nothing beyond human preferences make for the standard, right is reduced to might.

More recently, literary scholars have recognized the instability and inherent chaos of such a system and have tried to recover a sense of more objective values. In a recent opinion piece for *The Chronicle of Higher Education*, for example, Eric Bennett bemoans the current state of American political discourse and lays the blame at the feet of humanities departments' shift away from value questions in the 1980s.[22] No longer was the field "rigorously defined." Instead, it opened up to "the local, the little, the recent, and the demotic."[23] Bennett emphasizes that along with the democratization of the canon came a rejection of the English discipline's authority. By "equat[ing] expertise with power and power with oppression and malicious advantage," he argues, English departments left the liberal arts undefended in the face of economic and political pressures that reduce human life, meaning, and value to the pragmatic and material.[24]

Bennett concludes his reflections with a charge to reinvigorate the English discipline by exercising "modes of expression slow enough to inoculate against [the] flimsy thinking" so prevalent, and destructive, today. The stakes, he says, could not be higher—not only for the academy, which needs good literary critics, but also for the country, which is in "mortal need of good citizens." While Bennett's critique of contemporary literary studies is laudable, without the sturdy foundations available through Christian convictions, such a return to humanistic study seems destined merely to put us on the same course as Arnold set us on a hundred and fifty years ago. Christians need great literature. And if the field is to retain its enchantment, resounding redemptive notes, and taste for enchantment, literary study needs Christians. There is perhaps no better place for such work than in Christian liberal arts colleges, where both the students and the discipline can be brought under the lordship of Christ and governed by his purposes.

[1] Shirley Jackson, "The Lottery," *Literature: An Introduction to Reading and Writing*, 7th ed., eds. Edgar V. Roberts and Henry E. Jacobs (Upper Saddle River, NJ: Pearson, 2004), 245-250.

[2] Ruth Franklin, "'The Lottery' Letters," *The New Yorker*, June 25, 2013, https://www.newyorker.com/books/page-turner/the-lottery-letters./

[3] Ibid.

[4] Ibid.

[5] Greg Johnson and Thomas R. Arp, *Perrine's Literature: Structure, Sound & Sense*, 13th ed. (Boston: Cengage, 2018), 708.

[6] *Britannica Academic*, s.v. "Eagle," accessed March 12, 2019, https://academic-eb-com.ezproxy.liberty.edu/levels/collegiate/article/eagle/31700.

[7] Alfred, Lord Tennyson, "The Eagle," in *Perrine's Literature: Structure, Sound & Sense*, 708.

[8] C. S. Lewis, "Meditations in a Toolshed," *God in the Dock* (Grand Rapids, MI: Eerdmans, 1970), 212-215.

[9] Horace, *The Art of Poetry*, in *The Critical Tradition*, shorter 3rd ed., ed. David Richter (New York: St. Martin's, 2016), 75-85.

[10] Luci Shaw, "Beauty and the Creative Impulse," *The Christian Imagination* (Colorado Springs, CO: Shaw Books, 2002), 94. Shaw's insight resonates with J. R. R. Tolkien's discussion of the realm of Faerie, especially in his essay "On Fairy-Stories," in *The Tolkien Reader* (New York: Del Ray, 1986), 33-99.

[11] Basil, *Address to Young Men on the Right Use of Greek Literature* 3.

[12] C. S. Lewis, *The Screwtape Letters* (London: Centenary Press, 1944), 69.

[13] David Lyle Jeffrey and Gregory Maillet, *Christianity and Literature* (Downers Grove, IL: InterVarsity Academic, 2011), 87.

[14] Susan Gallagher and Roger Lundin, *Literature through the Eyes of Faith* (New York: Harper Collins, 1989), xxiv.

[15] Samuel Coleridge, *Biographia Literaria*, in *The Norton Anthology of Theory and Criticism*, 2d ed., ed. Vincent Leitch, *et al.* (New York: Norton, 2010), 584-591.

[16] Robert Merrihew Adams, *Finite and Infinite Goods: A Framework for Ethics* (Oxford: Oxford University Press, 2002), 4.

[17] Ibid., 89.

[18] Ibid., 189.

[19] Gene Edward Veith, *Reading between the Lines* (Wheaton, IL: Crossway, 1990), 46.

[20] Adams, 4.

[21] Terry Eagleton, *Literary Theory: An Introduction* (Minneapolis: University of Minnesota Press, 2008), 10.

[22] Eric Bennett, "Dear Humanities Profs: We Are the Problem," *Chronicle of Higher Education*, April 13, 2018, https://www.chronicle.com/article/Dear-Humanities-Profs-We-Are/243100.

[23] Ibid.

[24] Ibid.

6

HISTORY IS GOOD
FOR THE SOUL

*Finding Flourishing Through
Studying the Past*

Mark D. Janzen

"HISTORY IS MORE OR LESS BUNK." THOSE
infamous words belong to automobile pioneer Henry Ford, for
whom the only useful history is "the history we make today."[1]
Countless students echo Ford's sentiments, regarding history
classes as the pointless memorization and regurgitation of facts
having little bearing on their lives. High school graduates commonly recall their history classes as irrelevant and boring, leading them to ask why they had to study history at all.[2]

Moreover, given the widespread prioritization of STEM
classes over history and other liberal arts, it must be asked
whether history deserves its secondary status. Is the study of the
past less important than other fields of study? Was Henry Ford

right, or should history stand alongside other fields of study in the liberal arts tradition as foundational for human flourishing? I want to make the case that the modern tendency to minimize the importance of studying history is misleading because when properly taught, studied, and appreciated, history is revealed to be integral to the liberal arts. It is essential, in fact, for human flourishing and developing well-ordered souls. History complements and aids our understanding of important intellectual pursuits—philosophy, theology, science, to name a few—and informs to a great extent what it is to be human.

THE TASKS OF HISTORY

History is "the art of reconstructing the past,"[3] of "bringing the past to life—or *resurrecting* it."[4] Done properly, the discipline of history—with its interpretation and application of data from primary sources—is *exciting*! It's hardly the mere regurgitation of facts. History done well means "exploring ... the ways people in distant ages constructed their lives," and this "involves a sense of beauty and excitement, and ultimately another perspective on human life and society."[5] The best historians craft instructive narratives that confront us with the past—with all its comforts as well as its challenges and lessons.

It's important to distinguish between "history" and "the past." The past encompasses an inexhaustible set of dates, facts, events, and individuals, most of which are irretrievable. C. S. Lewis likened the past to a roaring waterfall churning out billions of facts and events, "any one of them too complex to grasp in its entirety, and the aggregate beyond all imagination."[6] For this reason, studying the past requires the construction of a thoughtful narrative. Perhaps superficial presentations of history as a random collection of disjointed facts explains why many students do not appreciate history.

One hallmark characteristic of modernity is its tendency toward parochialism, that is, its tendency to ignore the wisdom and perspectives on flourishing on offer from previous generations. Gaining these perspectives, however, is one of the great benefits of studying history. The best historians are storytellers whose stories explore the human experience. The past, of course, is "as chaotic, uncoordinated, and complex as life itself," and history is about bringing some sense of order to that chaos. These are not fictitious but true stories, based on evidence from the past but presented in an "interesting, coherent, and useful narrative."[7]

Just as an artist selects his or her subject, paint, canvas, and so on, so too the historian engages in a series of choices when studying the past. History writing is a selective process, for the past, with its innumerable events and circumstances, is simply too vast to fully recapture. For example, after witnessing firsthand the appalling carnage of the American Civil War, Walt Whitman wrote in his notes, "The real war will never get in the books."[8] Whitman recognized the impossibility of accurately capturing all the sordid details of the Civil War. Rather than making the vocation of history useless, Whitman's quote highlights its importance. The past is not wholly unknowable, but the process of gaining historical knowledge is complicated. Since historians cannot directly observe the past like a scientist in a lab, they study the vestiges of a vanished reality: phantoms, echoes, and fragments of lives long since passed.[9] Historians can retell only a fraction of all that has happened.

Despite the fact that historians make selective use of the past, possible interpretations of the past are not limitless. Historians' interpretations are limited by surviving evidence. Ignoring the standards of evidence amounts to leaving history for fiction. Historians are tasked with cobbling together a wide range of sources, requiring them to interpret evidence, evaluate claims and counterclaims, possess the creativity to craft compelling evidence-based narratives, and so on. Such skills, of course, are central to a number of disciplines, particularly within the liberal arts. The application of these analytical thinking skills to the wisdom of the past makes history distinct.

Each of the liberal arts is connected broadly to history, as historical circumstances and context shape the study of a host of those disciplines. How could one properly understand the writings of Charles Dickens, for instance, without some knowledge of the Industrial Revolution? Tracing the development of thought on a particular topic in the Great Books tradition requires an ability to think historically. Humanity's greatest thinkers were informed by the history of ideas. History helps us understand those ideas.

HISTORY AND PRESENT SOCIETY: IT'S COMPLICATED

Contrary to the negative experiences of some high school history students, studying the past is revelatory and often transformative! Because the past invades our present life in a host of unavoidable ways that speak to the very essence of humanity, the historian's task extends beyond the academy. Much of the linkage between past and present strikes to the core of what it is to be human. Societies speak languages inherited from the past. They embrace (or reject) religions, traditions, and customs that originate in the past. People use technology they did not invent. Even the human genome has a history! One cannot escape the past's invasion of the present. Whether we like it or not, the past holds the key to understanding the present.

Unfortunately, sometimes this interest in the past is merely trivial. A passing interest in the past is evident in the popularity of movies, television shows, and video games set in the past, the existence of the so-called "History" channel, and the continual presence of history books on the *New York Times* bestsellers list. Sadly, most of this "history" is exaggeration at best and fiction at worst, rife with alternate histories and even aliens! We live in a time when knowledge of the past is viewed with increasing skepticism or indifference as the culture revels in the present. Despite having a wealth of knowledge at our fingertips via devices in our pockets and purses, our collective knowledge of and interest in *factual* history has perhaps never been lower.

THE HISTORICAL PATH TO FLOURISHING

One casualty of society's fleeting interest in the past is our ability to think *deeply* about the past.[10] We must reverse this trend, not least because this ability encourages our growth in intellectual virtues that are crucial to human flourishing.

Being inspired by others sparks within us the desire to flourish, and few things rival the past's power to inspire us. As Fea wonderfully summarizes:

> The past has the power to stimulate us, fill us with emotion, and arouse our deepest convictions about what is good and right. When we study inspirational figures of the past, we often connect with them through time and leave the encounter wanting to be better people or perhaps even continue their legacy of reform, justice, patriotism, or heroism.[11]

We are motivated by the great deeds of yesteryear, many of them memorialized in film and literature—the heroism of the Allies storming the beaches at Normandy or the iconic planting of the American flag on Iwo Jima less than a year later. Figures like William Wilberforce, Nelson Mandela, and Martin Luther King, Jr. inspire us in their efforts to end slavery or racial discrimination. Studying such examples prompts us to act similarly in furtherance of God's shalom.

In studying the past we're inspired to great deeds, but we're also invited to join the vibrant conversation of Great Ideas. The writings of Plato, Aristotle, Augustine, Thomas Aquinas, Thomas Paine, Isaac Newton, Johannes Kepler, and countless other philosophers, theologians, scientists, and authors move us to think deeply about our world, our place in it, and our relationship to God. They invite us to connect with them through the timeless truths they espouse, and by expanding our minds and helping us define our morals and find our place in the world. They allow us to conquer the constant temptation to think only of the here and now. C. S. Lewis terms this *chronological snobbery*, "the uncritical acceptance of the intellectual climate common to our own age and the assumption that whatever has gone out of date is on that account discredited."[12] Lewis rightly suggested that the best way to avoid such snobbery is to read an equal number of "old" and "new" books. Not only will this confront us with the wisdom of our predecessors, it will open us to "the books that will correct the characteristic mistakes of our own period."[13]

Just as history assists us in acquiring wisdom, it is beneficial for developing in virtue. Studying history both requires empathy and helps us develop it. Too often we seek to make the past work for us, rather than approaching it with "an attitude of wonder about what we might find and the kinds of people and ideas we might encounter."[14] Empathy is the virtue that safeguards against misappropriating the past. The past should not be approached seeking validation for our assumptions, especially considering the vastness of the past. A person with unscrupulous motives likely will find what they are looking for in the "study" of the past. The people and ideas from the past are not merely "talking points" for us to conjure up when it is convenient to justify our preconceived notions or political ideology. Instead, historical empathy is about understanding the mindsets and motivations of people from the past. Gaddis explains, "getting inside other people's minds requires that your own mind be open to their impressions—their hopes and fears, their beliefs and dreams, their sense of right and wrong, their perception of the world and where they fit in it."[15] Developing in empathy and overcoming chronological snobbery go a long way toward growing our ability to flourish alongside others.

Historical empathy is an intellectual and imaginative activity simultaneously requiring discipline and a certain level of intellectual maturity.[16] In short, it demands a willingness to listen and learn. History is a great teacher of empathy, yet the lessons imparted extend beyond the study of the past. The skills with which we develop historical empathy also cultivate within us empathy for our neighbors today. The study of history helps fulfill education's true aim: the growth of the whole person. This enables us to flourish as human beings; with such an understanding, history is anything but boring, useless, irrelevant, or bunk.

THINKING CHRISTIANLY ABOUT THE PAST

Not only is history good for the soul in helping us flourish as beings created in the image of God, but Christianity itself is firmly rooted in history. Redemption takes place on the stage of history: the atonement of sins required a specific, historical act. If the crucifixion and resurrection of Jesus Christ are not historical, then there is no Christianity. As Paul reminds the Corinthians, "if Christ has not been raised, your faith is futile and you are still in your sins" (1 Cor. 15:17, ESV). Christianity champions a linear history initiated by God's creation of the heavens and the earth, redeemed by the cross and resurrection, and culminating in the future return of Christ.

Far more than an intellectual exercise, the Christian's study of history should be rooted in love, even for those long dead, as an extension of the call to love one's neighbors.[17] Far removed from the "history-as-ammunition" approach popular in contemporary political discourse, history done well values the individuals studied as fellow divine image bearers.[18] But how do we love those who have come before? This type of love is not sentimental, idealistic, or self-serving. As Oliver O'Donovan explains, this type of love, "whatever actions it gives rise to, is contemplative in itself, rejoicing in the fact that its object is there, not wanting to do anything 'with' it."[19] Past individuals and societies had their own ways of living, their own perspectives on life, and their own emotions and hopes. As best it can, history must seek to understand those ways of living and those perspectives as they really were, and only afterwards attempt to glean lessons for the present. When we approach the past simply to solve our own problems, we treat individuals from the past as mere *things*, as tools to be used rather than as beings made in God's image. In the process, we risk sinning, for the "propensity to treat human beings as things" lies at the heart of many sins.[20]

History clearly demonstrates the reality and consequences of human sin, revealing time and again that we live in a broken, violent, and unjust world. When it comes to human nature, there is a strong interplay between theology and history. Recognition of the devastating reality of living in a sinful world helps us make some sense of the atrocities committed by the likes of Nero, Hitler, and Stalin. Such an understanding enables us to point out injustice and judge atrocities, but its application goes deeper still. Understanding the reality of sin allows us to "maintain a healthy skepticism about movements in the past committed to utopian ends, unlimited progress, or idealistic solutions to the problems of this world."[21] The doctrine of sinfulness explains the universal human condition that history evidences—our search for meaning; our struggle with power and pride; our terrible tendency to harm each other and ourselves, sometimes on a nearly incomprehensibly tragic scale. Properly done, the study of history reinforces the words of Augustine to God: "our heart is restless until it rests in you."[22]

The Christian's study of history also should be approached with humility, being mindful of Paul's warning that knowledge puffs up (1 Cor. 8:1). We can understand only a fraction of the past, and this should leave us marveling at the God of history.

To make any sense of the past, we must selectively simplify, organize, and categorize historical information. A lack of awareness of this can lead to an exaggeration of our mastery of history, making God's mastery of it less wondrous.[23] The proper approach finds a mean within this tension, making well-reasoned and factual claims about the past while retaining a humble attitude.

Thinking Christianly about the past is essential to Christian growth. History allows us to marvel at the omniscience of God and the unfolding of his redemptive plan. It helps us fulfill the call to love our neighbors by respecting those who lived in the past, while reinforcing the importance of humility in the presence of an awe-inspiring God.

HISTORY AND CIVIC DUTY

It is also instructive to understand the importance of history as citizens of a democratic republic. A 2003 Gallop survey of 1,008 American adults reveals alarming deficiencies in our knowledge of the past. Over half the respondents (53%) did not know that the first ten amendments to the U.S. Constitution are known as the Bill of Rights. Roughly two-thirds (67%) did not know that Martin Luther King, Jr. is the author of "Letter from a Birmingham Jail." Less than half (42%) could not name the national anthem.[24] Such data is disheartening because it indicates the erosion of America's system of representative democracy; indeed, when societies detach themselves from history they soon find themselves adrift from collective flourishing, drifting toward disarray.

Ignorance of history creates a form of cultural near-sightedness and chronological snobbery, a danger that is all too obvious in modern political discourse. Political "hot takes" often lead directly to historical questions. For example, discussions about welfare inevitably turn to arm-chair analyses about past initiatives like the "New Deal" from the 1940s or the "Great Society" from the 1960s. Historical evidence is not the only factor in such debates, but it is clear that politicians and pundits are fond of appropriating the past to suit their present needs. This should not be. As McKenzie notes, "as citizens of a free society, called to exercise a voice in the public square, our historical ignorance leaves us vulnerable."[25] Knowledge of history is therefore one of the prerequisites of being a good citizen and guardian of values.

Genuine citizenship rests on a bedrock of history. More than any other field of study, history attempts to explain the complexities behind how societies came to be, as well as how they interact. It also seeks to provide the information necessary to make wise decisions when voting, instituting policies, or evaluating their effectiveness. As Stearns notes, "History provides data about the emergence of national institutions, problems, and values—it's the only significant storehouse of such data available."[26] The study of history allows a voting public to understand the causal relationship between past laws and actions and their attendant consequences, which is crucial to voting wisely. More importantly, studying history encourages "habits of the mind" that are essential for public behavior and civic discourse, regardless of whether one is a leader, voter, or simple observer.[27]

AN ATTEMPT AT WHAT HENRY FORD REALLY MEANT

History is *not* bunk. Henry Ford's famous comment was motived by his belief that the U.S. should not intervene in World War I. He felt people were using history unscrupulously to justify intervention. In truth, Ford's relationship with history was complicated. Certainly he valued the innovations of the present more than the lessons of the past, but he also constructed over one hundred buildings to house the Henry Ford Museum, which is dedicated to the history of American inventions and traditions.[28]

What exactly Ford meant by his infamous comment remains obscure, but he attempted to clarify his meaning some years later: "History as taught in the schools deals largely with wars, political controversies.... When I went to our history books to learn how our forefathers harrowed the land, I discovered the historians knew nothing about harrows. Yet our country depended more on harrows than great speeches."[29] While this might be empty rationalization, it appears Ford wanted more from history than he had been taught. He longed for something that taught a deeper lesson, something that he could apply to his humanity, something that would truly *educate*. History as arbitrary, empty facts is the history that Ford said was bunk—and I am inclined to agree! However, history with a focus on human flourishing—that is, history done well—is far from bunk. Studying history inspires and motivates us. It produces empathy and other virtues, and it is vital for understanding God's redemption of humanity. It is, in short, good for the soul.

---

[1] Both of Ford's quotes are from "Fight to Disarm His Life's Work, Henry Ford Vows," interview by Charles N. Wheeler, *Chicago Tribune*, May 25, 1916.

[2] John Fea, *Why Study History? Reflecting on the Importance of the Past* (Grand Rapids, MI: Baker Academic, 2013), 28-29. This excellent treatment of the importance of studying the past is written from a Christian perspective and is a tremendously helpful resource for thinking Christianly about history.

[3] Fea, *Why Study History?*, 3.

[4] John Tosh, *The Pursuit of History*, 3d ed. (New York: Longman, 2002), 7.

[5] Peter Stearns, "Why Study History? (1998)," *American Historical Association*, accessed March 1, 2019, https://www.historians.org/about-aha-and-

membership/aha-history-and-archives/historical-archives/why-study-history-(1998).

6 C. S. Lewis, "Historicism," in *Christian Reflections*, ed. Walter Hooper (Grand Rapids, MI: Eerdmans, 1967), 107.

7 John H. Arnold, *History: A Very Short Introduction* (New York: Oxford University Press), 13.

8 Quoted in Robert Tracy McKenzie, *The First Thanksgiving: What the Real Story Tells Us about a Loving God and Learning from History* (Downers Grove, IL: IVP Academic, 2013), 25-26.

9 Ibid., 26.

10 McKenzie, *The First Thanksgiving*, 10.

11 Fea, *Why Study History?*, 30.

12 C.S. Lewis, *Surprised by Joy: The Shape of my Early Life* (New York: Harcourt Brace Jovanovich, 1956), 207.

13 C.S. Lewis, Preface to *On the Incarnation*, by St. Athanasius (Yonkers, NY: St. Vladimir's Seminary Press, 2011), 10-11.

14 Fea, *Why Study History?*, 58-59.

15 John Lewis Gaddis, *The Landscape of History: How Historians Map the Past* (New York: Oxford University Press, 2002), 124.

16 Fea, *Why Study History?*, 58-59.

17 Beth Barton Schweiger, "Seeing Things: Knowledge and Love in History," in *Confessing History: Explorations in Christian Faith and the Historian's Vocation*, ed. John Fea, Jay Green, and Eric Miller (Notre Dame, IN: University of Notre Dame Press, 2010), 60-80.

18 McKenzie, *The First Thanksgiving*, 17.

19 Oliver O'Donovan, *Common Objects of Love: Moral Reflection and the Shaping of Community* (Grand Rapids, MI: Eerdmans, 2002), 16.

20 McKenzie, *The First Thanksgiving*, 17.

21 Fea, *Why Study History?*, 91.

22 Augustine, *Confessions* 1.1. See also the excellent treatment in Fea, *Why Study History?*, 89-93.

23 McKenzie, *The First Thanksgiving*, 18-19.

[24] George H. Gallup, Jr., "How Many Americans Know History, Part 1," Gallup, October 21, 2003, accessed February 11, 2019, https://news.gallup.com/poll/9526/how-many-americans-know-us-history-part.aspx.

[25] McKenzie, *The First Thanksgiving*, 12.

[26] Sterns, "Why Study History?"

[27] Ibid.

[28] "The Henry Ford Museum and Greenfield Village (The Edison Institute)," Michigan.gov, accessed February 11, 2019, https://www.michigan.gov/mshda/0,4641,7-141-54317_19320_61909_61927-54578--,00.html.

[29] Arthur Van Vlissingen, Jr., "The Idea Behind Greenfield," *The American Legion Monthly* 13.4 (1932): 7.

7

LIVING WORDS

*The Arts of Grammar and Rhetoric
According to C. S. Lewis*

Melinda Nielsen and Hannah Rogers

IN A WORLD INUNDATED BY MESSAGES AND branding, every word matters. What we say and how we say it powerfully influences how others perceive us, whether through social media, personal networking, oral presentations, or formal writing. The aim of language arts—traditionally known as the study of grammar and rhetoric—is that each student learns to pick and choose the best words, to arrange ideas logically and elegantly, and to communicate their message engagingly.

THE DIGNITY OF WORDS

Beyond their everyday function, words have a special significance—indeed, a God-given dignity—for Christians. God sent
his Son as the Word and chooses to communicate through words
in Scripture. Accordingly, God ennobles human language to participate in His self-giving love. The Psalmist remarks, "How precious to me are your thoughts, O God! How vast is the sum of
them! Were I to count them, they would outnumber the grains of
sand" (Psalm 139:17-18, NIV). The Incarnation of Christ is the instance of complete divine speech through which Christ reveals
to mankind the innermost thoughts of God. The beginning of the
Gospel of John speaks of this: "In the beginning was the Word,
and the Word was with God, and the Word was God.... The
Word became flesh and made his dwelling among us. We have
seen his glory, the glory of the One and Only son, who came from
the Father, full of grace and truth" (John 1:1, 14, NIV). In Jesus,
the incommunicable is communicated to mankind, for Christ, the
Word of God, speaks to us of the full glory of God. The eternal
Word by which God fashioned all of creation becomes physically
present to mankind, Emmanuel, "God with us." As Jesus himself
states: "Anyone who has seen me has seen the Father" (John 14:9,
NIV). Through Jesus, God has fully opened the lines of communication between God and man.

The incarnation not only gives God's Word to man, but
through the God-man, gives man the ability to respond to that
Word. And so Christ teaches that we "may ask [him] for anything in my name, and [he] will do it" (John 14:14, NIV). Christ
reveals a model for prayer in the Sermon on the Mount; at Pen-
tecost, the diversity of human language is made the bearer of the
Gospel; in Scripture, human writing itself participates in God's
self-revelation, as "living and active, sharper than any two-
edged sword (Heb. 4.12, ESV). Because of Christ's manifestation
of the divine mind, man can communicate with God in a direct
and meaningful way.

In this way, the words we use and the structure of our speech have eternal significance, for they are an important aspect of our participation in God's created order. Christ, as the Word of God, has given us the proper means of communication with God and has shown us how language might be restored and again used in joyful appreciation of our creator. As a result, no act of communication is a casual affair, but rather an opportunity that either contributes to shalom or perpetuates falsehood and folly. Our speech, when utilized properly, possesses a new dignity: it is able to increase human flourishing by moving our souls and those around us closer to God.

Among modern communicators, few Christians have used words more effectively than C. S. Lewis. Today, over fifty years after his death, his books have sold more than 200,000 million copies and their popularity shows no signs of waning. His writings are not only renowned for their lucidity and logic but have spoken powerfully to diverse readers, ranging from atheists to schoolchildren. As such, Lewis demonstrates the life-giving potential of language and rhetoric, yet his writings also show that such impact is the result not of good luck or even innate ability. Rather, Lewis intentionally apprenticed himself to the craft of reading and writing, of grammar and rhetoric—and we can do so, too.

GRAMMAR AND THE ART OF SEEING

Lewis's writings and example harness the power of classical grammar and rhetoric and can help us to reimagine their pivotal role in liberal arts education. When we hear the term "grammar," we may think of torturous sentence diagraming or fixing apostrophes or capitalization. However, rightly understood, grammar is far more than the memorization of arbitrary rules. For Lewis, the study of grammar is learning the value and meaning of each word; choosing exactly the right phrase; perceiving the relations between words, things, and ideas as we craft each phrase; and arranging language to represent our thoughts exactly. It's the art of saying no more and no less than is in your mind. If a person says, "I know what I mean but I can't put it into words," he probably does not really know quite what he means, or at least does not have the tools to articulate it clearly.

The study of grammar, then, begins with understanding the power of words. No one word is exactly the same as another; each has its own feel, weight, and connotation. Just as marble is the raw material of sculpture, words are the raw material of grammar, and as Lewis notes, "words, like every other medium, have their own proper powers and limitations."[1] Moreover, words are the true foundation of any liberal arts education, as clarity of language promotes clarity of thought and self-knowledge; as Wormwood gloats in *The Screwtape Letters*, "of course we have contrived that their very language should be all smudge and blur; what would be a bribe in someone else's profession is a tip or a present in theirs."[2] Learning to find and use the right word is like becoming a good chef. Through recipes, experimentation, and continual practice, a person learns the flavor and capacity of each ingredient, becoming free to improvise so as to create a wholesome meal.

Such apprenticeship to the craft of words, however, need not be a laborious task, burdened by dictionaries and thesauruses. Rather, in the model of liberal education, it is by encountering words in good and great literature over and over again that a person learns to appreciate just what words are capable of. Such encounters first take place during solitary reading, later bearing fruit in conversation with friends or in a classroom where students and teacher together read out loud, ponder, and push to the limit the implications of each word. Such a careful habit of mind forms the only sure foundation for all reading, from Shakespeare's plays to engineering manuals, for an understanding of grammar helps students learn to read generously and insightfully, giving preference to the value and integrity of the text on its own terms rather than what a clever reader can "make" of it. Grammar thus imparts a rigorous habit of mind which a person can then freely apply in a variety of ways and to a range of subjects, with the result that they may cultivate shalom wherever they find themselves later in life.

Because the study of grammar empowers a student to understand a text as accurately as possible, it also necessarily involves learning things that are external to the text. That is, since words represent things, actions, and ideas, we must also know something about the reality words represent in order to understand how to use them properly. Grammar, then, is not merely linguistic grammar, but includes foundational knowledge and context from a web of fields, from the "grammar" of history to the elements of physical science. To be ignorant of a work's context is to risk missing what is being said. Such knowledge, in turn, affects a person's ability to compose and share their message with others, for without careful attention to the meaning and contexts of words communication breaks down.

According to Lewis, a mind trained in the liberal arts by reading literature carefully is ready to see the things around him in their true light. That is, the close reader of texts "receives" the literature he is reading in a way that enables him humbly to inhabit another's mind. In *An Experiment in Criticism*, Lewis declares, "When we 'receive' [literature] we exert our sense and imagination and various powers according to the power of the artist."[3] That is, the trained reader will not attempt to twist a text to his own ideological ends, but rather will observe what the text actually says and patiently seek to understand the argument, narrative, or world set before him. Rigor of language—that is, seeking to understand on another's terms rather than one's own—trains the eyes and the senses, as well as the tongue. Thus, the study of grammar cultivates in students the virtuous ability to attend with love and humility to the circumstances and occupants of the world around them.

As the first and most foundational of the liberal arts, grammar's toolkit liberates the mind from ignorance so that it can read, see, and speak to others. Careful attention to the great authors of the past helps a student compose their own thoughts; if a student cannot see a text properly, he cannot hope to write one. By understanding foundational relations between words and ideas, grammar cultivates the ability to listen attentively to another's perspective, to understand it on its own terms, to do justice to other's ideas, and to find the best words to clothe one's own thoughts. Such skills contribute to the flourishing of the student by preparing one to participate in civil society, healthy citizenship, family life, and a lifetime of interacting with persons and perspectives beyond one's own preferences.

RHETORIC AND THE HEALTHY SOUL

Grammar alone, however, is not enough for effective communication; one must also learn to attend to the capacity of a particular audience. In short, one must study rhetoric. Like the term "grammar," the word "rhetoric" is commonly misused. Rhetoric is often seen as being, at best, the flourishes that help persuade another of one's position; we say sometimes, in this sense, that someone's words were "mere rhetoric." At worst, rhetoric can be misused through insincerity or even become an exercise in manipulation. However, rightly understood, rhetoric is the gracious and charitable effort to shape one's words to communicate fully with the exact audience one is addressing. It is the capstone that transforms the building blocks of grammar into a lasting edifice that can provide shelter and hospitality to enquirers, simultaneously teaching, delighting, and persuading, as Cicero explains.[4] Thus, the proper art and duty of rhetoric is to communicate the truth of the matter while simultaneously engaging the interests of the audience. Without genuine consideration for an audience, our words either disappear into a vacuum or, worse still, risk becoming manipulation. Properly understood, the study of rhetoric, then, requires self-examination as well as attention to the needs of the listener.

Aristotle's *Rhetoric* describes three primary ways of persuasion: arguments that stake their claim for truthfulness either in the speaker's character or *ethos*; arguments that appeal to the listener primarily through reason or *logos*; or arguments that move the emotions through *pathos* to assent to what is true. Together these three modes of persuasion engage the whole person in the search for and realization of truth. A student apprenticed to these three classical modes of persuasion and their offshoots will not only be able to argue a point effectively but will also be prepared to debate while respecting the dignity of others.

In character-based rhetoric, a writer or speaker may develop his claim to speak truthfully on the basis of personal credibility or the established integrity of another. The rhetorician effectively builds credibility by establishing personal character, giving evidence that he can be trusted to lead the audience in a fruitful direction. The study of rhetoric cannot, of course, by itself turn someone into a person of integrity. What it can do, though, is help an upright person learn how to craft thoughtful, truthful, and transparent arguments that are in keeping with upright character. An audience will not be persuaded by a speaker whom they cannot believe has their best interests in view. A speaker therefore becomes trustworthy when he knows his audience and acknowledges them as fellow souls with needs and desires that deserve to be taken into account.

Furthermore, the speaker must not only know the intended audience but also be able to use that knowledge to communicate clearly. As Aristotle states: "To write well, express yourself like the common people, but think like a wise man."[5] A truly effective rhetorician creates a rapport with the audience, using this connection to meet them where they are. When describing his project of evangelism and apologetics, Lewis explains how such rhetoric is essentially a type of translation: "My task was therefore simply that of a translator—one turning Christian doctrine, or what he believed to be such, into the vernacular, into language that unscholarly people would attend to and could understand."[6] As with translating, the writer or speaker must first grasp the idea, then render that idea into the form that will appeal to a specific audience. Thus, a good grounding in rhetoric gives one the resources to discover and adapt the best form with which to share ideas with an audience. Such attention and care for the needs of others shows how rhetoric has the potential not only to communicate a truthful message but, in so doing, also to become a way of loving one's neighbor. As students learn to properly consider their audience, they develop the ability to welcome their fellow human beings into an understanding of the true, the good, and the beautiful, thereby more effectively contributing to the flourishing of those around them.

If the ethos of rhetoric highlights the speaker's integrity and the credibility of their research, at its heart rhetoric's chief value is the way it cultivates our natural ability to understand and use logic persuasively. To write and speak effectively, a person must craft arguments that are sound, orderly, and attractive. Every email, every grant proposal, every brief, every sermon, stands or falls on how well it arranges and communicates a logical point. However, such rationality is more than an attractively added-on feature, for a true appeal to logic recognizes and honors the rational nature of the human person. In other words, a person cannot truly employ logos when he is deploying a veneer of cleverly phrased points to mask a fundamentally unsound claim. A person who can recognize an invalid argument sees through empty rhetoric and can construct rigorous arguments that do credit to the inherent rationality of the audience.

Moreover, the speaker not only has a responsibility to respect his own rationality but that of his audience. Too often rhetoric is debased into a way of persuading an audience to assent to something fundamentally unsound through suave speech. Such use is, as the philosopher Josef Pieper notes, both an abuse of language and an abuse of power that turns rhetoric into a weapon rather than a tool. Such rhetoric fails to see the person addressed as a fellow human being, instead operating as if the audience does not possess the reason necessary to counter the insufficient argument. As Pieper says, whoever addresses another person and "is in this guided by something other than the truth—such a person, from that moment on, no longer considers the other as partner, as equal. In fact, he no longer respects the other as a human person. From that moment on, to be precise, all conversation ceases; all dialogue and all communication come to an end."[7]

Without acknowledging that truth is the aim of rhetoric, the speaker may become a tyrant, behaving as if no one is capable of evaluating his claim. Such manipulation is easy for sinful human beings to slip into, and the brighter the student, the greater the temptation. However, careful grounding in the logos of rhetoric directs the student to be responsible in their use of persuasion, educating the student in logically rigorous habits of thought. Accordingly, when the speaker employs logos, he cooperates with the rational faculties of his audience so that they may seek the truth together.

The final classical means of persuasion is pathos, or engaging the audience's emotions in order to persuade. It may initially appear that emotional appeals are somehow inconstant with the emphasis on mankind's rational nature. However, as Lewis asserts, "One of the most important and effective uses of language is the emotional. It is also, of course, wholly legitimate. We do not talk only in order to reason or to inform. We have to make love and quarrel, to propitiate and pardon, to rebuke, console, intercede, and arouse."[8]

For Lewis, because mankind is a spirited creature, pathos is a valid means of persuasion. Indeed, it is not only valid, it is "lawful and necessary because, as Aristotle points out, intellect of itself 'moves nothing': the transition from thinking to doing, in nearly all men at nearly all moments, needs to be assisted by appropriate states of feeling."[9] Thus the liberal arts are not simply matters of cold logic; rather Christ-shaped liberal education guides the passions, recognizing them as a legitimate element of the human person so that grace may build on nature. As John Henry Newman observed, "the heart is commonly reached, not through the reason, but through the imagination, by means of direct impressions, by the testimony of facts and events, by history, by description. Persons influence us, voices melt us, looks subdue us, deeds inflame us."[10] Rhetoric acknowledges that, in addition to being rational animals, we are also "seeing, feeling, contemplating, [and] acting animal[s]."[11]

To be clear, rhetoric should seek not only to appeal to the passions but also to order or discipline them to correspond with reality. For not all appeals to emotion are appropriate. Just as with appeals to logic, pathos can seek to tell the truth or to lie. Thus, just as logos-based rhetoric draws the human person toward objective truth, pathos-based argument encourages us to grow in "objective sentiment." In *The Abolition of Man*, Lewis argues not merely that there is an objective natural law governing the universe, but the subtler point that there are objectively appropriate emotional responses to the universe, which require practice and training to function correctly.

Proper emotions correspond to the truth, and the teacher of pathos needs to serve the truth as much as does the teacher of logic. Accordingly, beautiful rhetoric, at the service of truth, participates in educating not only one's mind but also one's heart. By involving and educating the passions, Christ-shaped liberal education prevents the sort of intellectual deformity that Lewis laments: "it is not excess of thought but defect of fertile and generous emotion that marks them [the modern student] out. Their heads are no bigger than the ordinary: it is the atrophy of the chest beneath that makes them seem so."[12] For Lewis, modern educational experiments have created students who have no "chests" to do the heavy lifting on behalf of either reason or desire. Liberal learning cultivates students—not as mere workers, but as children of God.

Grammar and rhetoric engage the entire person in an authentic search for truth. Through the study of words, we learn how to listen and to see the world around us. Through ethos, we learn how to represent our character accurately, seeking to grow in credibility, to base authority in integrity, and to care for the needs and situation of our audiences. Through logos, we honor the value of human reason, rather than manipulating logic for selfish ends. Through pathos, we learn how to constructively include emotions in the search for truth, fostering a healthy and rational role for the passions. Together these elements engage the full soul of a person to seek and love the truth. This is especially noteworthy for Christians who recognize their responsibility to love God with their whole person, ordering every aspect of their soul to behold the truth, to live in harmony with others, to flourish with freedom as a son or daughter of God, and to cooperate with his providential plan. When used properly, classical language arts not only form students to read, write, and speak eloquently in whatever career they choose, but play an important role in freeing students to live in shalom as whole and healthy persons.

---

[1] C. S. Lewis, "Prudery and Philology," in *Present Concerns* (San Diego: Harvest Books, 2002), 88-89.

[2] C. S. Lewis, *The Screwtape Letters* (New York: HarperCollins, 2009), 191.

[3] C. S. Lewis, *An Experiment in Criticism* (New York: Cambridge University Press, 1996), 88.

[4] Cicero, *Orator* 69.

[5] Aristotle, *Poetics* xxii.4

6 C. S. Lewis, "Rejoinder to Dr. Pittenger," in *God in the Dock,* ed. Walter Hooper (Grand Rapids: Eerdmans, 1972), 183.

7 Josef Pieper, *Abuse of Language, Abuse of Power* (San Francisco: Ignatius Press, 1992), 21.

8 Lewis, *Studies in Words,* 314.

9 C. S. Lewis, *A Preface to Paradise Lost* (London: Oxford University Press, 1942), 52. See also Aristotle's *Nicomachean Ethics* VI.ii.5.

10 John Henry Newman, *Discussions and Arguments on Various Subjects* (London: Longmans, Green and Co., 1908), 293.

11 Newman, *Discussions and Arguments,* 294

12 Lewis, *The Abolition of Man,* 44.

8

A SEVENFOLD PICTURE

Virtues and the Good Life

Paul M. Gould

May I learn to love learning, O Lord,
for the world is yours,
and all things in it speak
—each in their way—of you:
of your mind,
your designs,
your artistry,
your power,
your unfolding purpose.

—A Liturgy for Students & Scholars[1]

WE FORMERLY LIVED JUST OUTSIDE THE CITY
limits of a small town west of Fort Worth, Texas. The city is
mostly composed of well-planned housing developments, full of
walking trails through former ranch land, dog parks, community
green spaces, and landscaped roundabouts. We would frequently drive to one of these planned communities to walk its
paths and enjoy its beauty. But outside these city limits, it may
as well be the wild west when it comes to urban planning. A
short walk from our door was a wedding chapel, a landscape
nursery, a water treatment plant, the local garbage business, a
cement mixing company, and a storage unit.

In my attempt to stay fit, I would run a route through this
conglomeration of commerce and industry. On many mornings,
I found myself dodging dump trucks, natural gas shipments,
hurried students barreling to the local high school, and parents
rushing off to work. The traffic added to my stress; the displaced
gravel and dust would clog my throat, obscure my vision, and
(undoubtedly) fill my lungs with unwanted particles. It's a tale
of two cities, we might say: one well-ordered, full of beauty, order, and abundance; the other, a random amalgamation of enti-
ties, producing discord, disharmony, and disgruntled runners.

This scenario strikes me as an apt metaphor for the contrast
between the traditional view of the university and its modern reality. On the traditional view, the university is organized around
a common vision of the good life (more on this below). Not so
today. There's no unifying principle to the modern university—
except perhaps the allure of wealth and status—and as a result,
it expands, in the words of Wendell Berry, "according to the principle of miscellaneous accretion, like a furniture storage business."[2] The modern university is like my old running route: a
fragmented series of warring factions competing for a slice of
market share on a dwindling patch of real estate next to a busy
highway.

These warring factions—the various disciplines and departments of the modern university—"have ceased to speak to each other."[3] Those factions (disciplines), usually within the sciences, that can demonstrate some real-world benefit are deemed "novel" or "cutting-edge" or "essential." Others, usually within the humanities, are often judged to be unnecessary leftovers of a bygone and less enlightened era. The goal of the modern university, according to Berry, is to make *"parts* of things": skilled engineers, skilled journalists, skilled computer programmers, and so on. [4] While students might gain skills to perform certain tasks, there is no guarantee that they will learn how to *live* well. The "part" made in computer science is disconnected from the "part" made in technical writing which is disconnected from the "part" made in calculus class. Little attention is given, however, to how these various "parts" of the modern self are supposed to fit together into a coherent and flourishing whole. It is entirely possible to excel in one area of life and fail miserably in another. Many do.

Contrast the modern picture with the traditional view of the university. Traditionally, knowledge is viewed as intrinsically valuable—valuable for its own sake—*and* for the benefits it brings. Importantly, all knowledge—all truths discovered—somehow illuminate and connect to the divine. Theology is the center, the hub, of all knowledge precisely because God is the source of all knowledge. The various domains of knowledge are the spokes. On this older view, the underlying idea of the university was "that good work and good citizenship are the inevitable by-products of the making of a good ... human being."[5] In other words, traditionally, the university exists for the making of humanity itself (and not just parts of things).

The university exists to convey knowledge and aid in the development of fully functioning—that is, virtuous—human beings. The result is order, abundance, harmony, and more as humans are nourished on the good, the true, and the beautiful. The Christian liberal arts college embraces this older way of thinking.

In this essay, I shall specify some of the ways a Christ-shaped liberal education can help develop virtue. In particular, I shall argue that a Christ-shaped liberal education can guide us in *making wise judgments, reordering loves and longings,* and *in living the true story of the world.* I begin by discussing the nature of virtue and the good life.

VIRTUE AND THE GOOD LIFE

If the university is for the making of humanity, our first question, then, must be: what is man? According to the philosopher Peter Kreeft, "There used to be maps, diagrams, pictures of a complete human being."[6] On this old way of thinking, there was an essence to man and a God-given purpose to life. The virtues were understood as qualities of character that aid us on our life's journey. This older way of thinking, along with its maps, diagrams, and pictures, have "fallen into disuse" and are widely thought to be relics of a less enlightened and more oppressive era in human history.[7] The dominant view today, especially in the secular university, is that there's no place for fixed essences or natures, purposes, or virtues (and vices). We've loosed ourselves from the shackles of religion. We are free to chart our own futures. We have reached a place where we can take our evolutionary future into our own hands. One day, we are told, our biology will be fused with our technology, and we will become transhuman. Eventually, we'll become posthuman. Something new. Something eternal, even.

There are at least two problems with this utopian vision. The first problem, to put it bluntly, is that it's false. Humans are not endlessly malleable. There is an essence to man, and this essence sets limits on who we are and what we can become. Man's modern "rage against the given" is rooted in idolatry and hubris. That's the second problem. This moral problem is the manifestation of one more epicycle of the root sin perpetrated by the first humans in the Garden of Eden: the desire to be like God.[8] As a result, modern man is empty, hollow at the core, and unhappy. Perhaps it is time to dust off the old maps, diagrams, and charts that detail the nature of the good life for humans. And what does one find? C. S. Lewis summarizes best. We find "the happiness that there is, not the happiness that is not."[9] And what is this happiness? "To be like God and to share His goodness in creaturely response."[10]

These old maps, diagrams, and charts are part and parcel of a Christ-shaped liberal arts education. In Christ, the apostle Paul tells us, "are hidden all the treasures of wisdom and knowledge" (Col 2:3, NIV). To enroll in a Christian liberal arts university or college is to sign up for a treasure hunt. Central to the Christian liberal arts vision is the idea that man is on a quest. We come into the world and take up our place in an on-going story. Our journey finds fulfillment as we organize our lives around the good that is God. This is the "X" on our map. The journey, of course, is full of danger and toil, trials and temptations. The virtues find their place as those stable and excellent qualities of character which enable the evils in life to be overcome, the tasks of the good life to be accomplished, and the journey to man's end to be completed.

Education in virtue is needed. The secular academy is wholly unfit to act as a moral educator, and so we must turn to the Christian liberal arts university or college.[11] For within these universities and colleges we find a vision for life that is true, good, and beautiful. We find not only a picture of human nature as it *is* and as it *ought* to be, but a map to help us along the way, as well. Without hyperbole, I say that as Christ-shaped liberal arts universities and colleges flourish, we all flourish. Central to this journey toward wholeness is the cultivation of the virtues and the right application of wise judgments. We turn now to explore how a liberal arts education *informs* us so that we might judge correctly.

MAKING WISE JUDGMENTS

It's not a stretch to say that there is a good bit of foolish activity and foolishness in our world today. Pretty much everywhere we find humans, we find folly: in politics, in sports, in entertainment, in education, even in religion. I'm not sure social media is helping in this area, either. Everyone is vying for attention, and so we're driven to do crazy—that is, foolish—things to garner "likes" or in the hopes that our video will go viral. I'm thinking in particular of things like the "bird-box" challenge, where folks blindfold themselves and walk around in public or the "tide pod" challenge where folks video themselves eating laundry detergent. These are foolish acts—and of course—they can be deadly, too.

Part of the problem is that many of us, perhaps most of us, are fixated (as C. S. Lewis puts it in his book *The Screwtape Letters*) "on the stream of immediate sense experiences."[12] We neither use our reasoning faculties very well, nor do we rightly perceive the sacred order of things, and so foolishness runs amok. We no longer know how to live wisely. When the fools are in charge, it's no surprise that our lives are often full of strife, discord, and anxiety. What is needed is a return to the virtue of wisdom.

Wisdom is one of four "cardinal" or "hinge" virtues from which all the other virtues in life hang. It is also the chief of the cardinal virtues because of its indispensable role in life. Only the wise person can be just, brave, and temperate (these being the remaining cardinal virtues). I define wisdom as understanding the sacred order of things and acting in accordance with this order. This definition of wisdom incorporates and enfolds the ancient insight that wisdom looks in two directions—or, as Joseph Pieper puts it: "perceptively it is turned toward reality" and "'imperatively' toward volition and action."[13] In other words, wisdom is concerned with both truth and conduct. My definition of wisdom also highlights the fact that humans are created according to a design plan, and so we flourish when we live the way God intended. When we insist on "going against the grain," as Jesus described Paul's pre-conversion mindset in Acts 26:14, foolishness and disintegration result. We want to understand the order of things and then apply this understanding in our daily life.

How can we become wise? A Christian liberal arts education can help. We learn about the sacred order of the world as we study in one hand the Scriptures, and in the other the canon of Western thought, all done in community under the guidance of a team of professors. We learn about the destructive nature of folly while reading about the rage of Achilles or the trials of Odysseus or the plunge into unfettered evil by Dr. Hyde. We grow in wisdom as we wrestle with ethical dilemmas raised by Moses or Paul or Hume or Kant. We see how ideas have consequences as we read de Tocqueville or Marx and consider our recent past. Most importantly, a Christian liberal arts education puts us on the path of wisdom, the path of life that finds its source in Christ.

REORDERING LOVES AND LONGINGS

There are three other virtues, according to the old maps: the theological virtues. These must be added to our four cardinal virtues to complete our picture of Man. While the four cardinal virtues are common to all and can be acquired through human effort, the theological virtues—faith, hope, and love—are infused virtues, gifted to us as we look to God as our highest good. Faith puts us on the path that leads to God and points us in the right direction. Hope stands between faith and love. Whereas faith helps us see the way, hope helps us walk the path. Hope is the "virtue of the wayfarer."[14] Love—God's love for man and man's love for God and his creation—perfects and gives all the other virtues shape as it directs them "toward the ultimate goal of union with God."[15]

A Christian liberal arts education helps us organize our lives around the good that is God. In reading the canon of Western literature, including the Bible, we learn three great truths: (1) that man's deepest desire is for God and a God-bathed world, (2) something has gone wrong: man is alienated from God, himself, and each other, and (3) we can't find our way back to God on our own. We learn that our condition is essentially defined as *status viatoris*, that is, as being "on the way."[16] We are pilgrims, *homo viators*, on a journey toward fulfillment. As creatures, our status is that of pilgrims who must navigate between the shores of being and nothingness, as we live in the "not yet" and press on toward the goal of human fulfillment, which on the Christian story can only be found through union with God.[17]

A question can be raised at this point, though. If entering into loving union with God is the center and summit of the Christian life, how does this claim fit with God's command to love our neighbors? If our highest good is friendship with God, does this not mean that we must turn our backs on others? The short answer is no (for the long answer, enroll in a Christian liberal arts college or university). Yes, we are to love God. It is, in fact, the deepest longing of the human heart to know and love him. The issue is not *whether* we love things other than God, but *how* we love them. We ought to love God *supremely*. But we ought not to love God *only*. We are to love things, as Augustine puts it, in their proper order. We can and do love things other than God: family, friends, work, play, our toys, and more besides. If we love each of these people or things as gifts from God that are to be enjoyed in creaturely response (and in their proper order according to their value), we love them rightly. If they occupy a place in our hearts that only God is meant to occupy, they quickly become idols.

When we begin to understand all of reality as a divine drama of wander and return to God, we see that true friendship with God must always unfold in love for others, too. While God is always our principle concern in love, still, as Aquinas puts it, "for his sake we love one another."[18] In loving others, we desire their flourishing as well as our own. That means that we must view others as fellow travelers and *friends* on the way, instead of as *strangers*. A Christian liberal arts education brings together fellow travelers, who jointly walk the path of faith, in hope, toward an everlasting love.

LIVING THE TRUE STORY OF THE WORLD

"Our hearts," writes James K. A. Smith, "traffic in stories."[19] We love stories. We live as part of a story. Our actions find meaning, and we find an identity, within some overarching story that inspires and shapes our hearts. But which story? There are many stories that compete for our allegiance and invite our participation. Education in the dominant thought of the Western world will acquaint students with certain stories: naturalism, hedonism, materialism, gnosticism, romanticism, idealism, atheism, narcissism, consumerism, totalitarianism, socialism, capitalism, pantheism, panentheism, and of course, Christian theism. Asking, of all these competing stories, which one is both true to the way the world is and true to the way the world ought to be, is of supreme importance. There is a true story of the world. And it's the best story. It's the best possible story. In this, the Christian story, you find the living God who, in love, spreads his joy and delight in creating this good world. You find a God who pursues when we run. You find Jesus, who offered his life so that we could find forgiveness from sins and our way home. And you find a sevenfold picture of human flourishing to help guide your steps along the way. Do you want to live a great life? Do you want to live for something bigger than yourself? Then take up your place in the gospel story and enroll in a Christian liberal arts college or university that is in the business of making humanity itself.

1 Douglas Kaine McKelvey, *Every Moment Holy* (Nashville, TN: Rabbit Room Press, 2017), 38.

2 Wendell Berry, "The Loss of the University," in *Home Economics* (New York: North Point, 1987), 76.

3 Ibid.

4 Ibid, 77.

5 Ibid., 77.

6 Peter Kreeft, *Back to Virtue* (San Francisco, CA: Ignatius Press, 1992), 15.

7 Ibid.

8 This idea, including the modernist posture of "rage against the given" is discussed in Joel Thompson, "Transhumanism: How Far is Too Far?" *The New Bioethics* 23:2 (2017): 169-172.

9 C. S. Lewis, *The Problem of Pain* (New York: HarperCollins, 2001), 47.

10 Ibid.

11 See Alasdair MacIntyre, *After Virtue* (Notre Dame, IN: University of Notre Dame Press, 1981), 195.

12 C. S. Lewis, *The Screwtape Letters* (Westwood, NJ: Barbour Books, 1990), 12.

13 Josef Pieper, *The Four Cardinal Virtues* (Notre Dame, IN: University of Notre Dame Press, 1966), 12.

14 Charles Pinches, "On Hope," in *Virtues and Their Vices*, eds. Kevin Timpe and Craig A. Boyd (Oxford: Oxford University Press, 2014), 362.

15 William C. Mattison, *Introducing Moral Theology* (Grand Rapids: Brazos, 2008), 302, quoted in Karen Swallow Prior, *On Reading Well* (Grand Rapids: Brazos, 2018), 143.

16 Joseph Pieper, *Faith, Hope, Love* (San Francisco: Ignatius Press, 1992), 91.

17 Ibid., 96.

18 *Summa Theologica*, II-II.23.5ad 1; quoted in Paul J. Wadell, "Charity: How Friendship with God unfolds in Love for Others," in *Virtues and Their Vices*, 381.

19 James K. A. Smith, *Imagining the Kingdom* (Grand Rapids: Baker, 2013), 108.

9

UNITY OF KNOWLEDGE AND UNITY WITH GOD

Theology's Crucial Place in Education

Greg Peters

IN THE LATE TWENTIETH CENTURY, WHEN higher education became redefined as a commodity or product, bought and sold for the purpose of immediate employment, colleges and universities came to regard the study of theology as worth very little. Theology, it was thought, is impractical. Pointless for all, save future ministers. Now, in the twenty-first century, such thinking has become commonplace. In a day when studying *philosophy* is often dismissed as "useless" (and it often is), then how much more a course or a degree in theology!

Moreover, how did theology ever find itself among the liberal arts in the first place? Should theology even have a place at the higher education table these days? Is it even necessary or possible to defend theology's place in the academy when discussing a Christ-shaped liberal arts education? In other words, can theology be taken for granted in a Christian context? Are not all the liberal arts taught at a Christian university so impregnated with the integration of theology and Scripture that classes devoted to theology are superfluous for anyone other than those declaring theology and/or biblical studies their major?

If some of these questions appear wildly off base, consider this: even the Roman Catholic theologian John Henry Newman had to defend the place of theology among the liberal arts when casting his vision for a *Roman Catholic* university in predominantly Roman Catholic Ireland. "A University," he writes in *The Idea of a University*, "I should lay down, by its very name professes to teach universal knowledge: Theology is surely a branch of knowledge: how then is it possible for it to profess all branches of knowledge, and yet to exclude from the subjects of its teaching" theology?[1] A great question indeed.

THEOLOGY'S ENTRY INTO CHRISTIAN EDUCATION

Theology, as an area of study or academic discipline, does not originate in a Christian context. The first use of the word "theology" actually comes from the ancient Greek philosopher Socrates, quoted by his student Plato, "But what precisely are the patterns for theology or stories about the gods?" he asks his interlocutor Adeimantus.[2] Socrates rejects the vision of the gods presented by the poets (e.g., Homer), insisting that his way of talking about gods (*theologias* in Greek) is correct. With Socrates, Aristotle also rejects the theology of the poets.[3]

Although some Christian writers of the earliest centuries were hesitant to use the word "theology," choosing instead to think of themselves as philosophers (i.e., lovers of God's wisdom), by the time of Augustine of Hippo theology was understood as "reason or discourse concerning divinity."[4] Mostly in these early centuries, "theology" was scriptural interpretation. For example, Origen of Alexandria wrote, Jesus "revealed to his true disciples the nature of God and told them about His characteristics. We find traces of these in the scriptures and make them the starting-points of our theology."[5]

By the medieval era theology was still mostly thought of as biblical commentary, especially in the monasteries.[6] But as the universities started to develop around the year 1200, the subject of theology began to undergo a change. By the mid-twelfth century the word *theologia* was used to refer to theology as an academic discipline. In this sense theology was no longer just biblical commentary but had come to mean "a scientific model of understanding the faith as a tool for the education of the professional clerical class."[7] In other words, theology began to take on the connotations that we associate with it today when we think of it as an academic discipline among the Christian liberal arts. Yet, early medieval thinkers did not consider theology *one of* the liberal arts: the seven liberal arts were themselves regarded as preparation for the discipline of theology.[8] Theology was the "queen of the sciences/arts," if you will.

The great Franciscan theologian Bonaventure is a good example of how theology came to be viewed among those associated with the new universities. As an academic field of study, theology needed to find its seat at the academic table, and theologians like Bonaventure justified theology's place not just at the table but at the head of the table. In his *Collations on the Seven Gifts of the Holy Spirit*, based on conferences given at the University of Paris in 1268, Bonaventure turns to a discussion of knowledge. He says there are four radiances of knowledge: philosophical, theological, grace, and glory. Concerning the first two, he writes, "the radiance of philosophical knowledge is great in the view of worldly people, but it is slight in comparison with the radiance of Christian knowledge. And the radiance of theological knowledge seems slight in the view of worldly people, but in reality, it is great."[9]

In other words, theology's radiance is greater than philosophy's though they are both gifts from God. "Philosophical knowledge," writes Bonaventure, "is nothing other than the certain knowledge of truth in as far as it can be investigated. Theological knowledge is the pious knowledge of truth as believable."[10] Further, philosophical knowledge is of three kinds: natural, rational, moral. In short, all knowledge that we can now think of as the liberal arts falls under "philosophical knowledge." But these areas of knowledge are not pagan in contradistinction to theology proper. In fact, Bonaventure concludes that "anyone who has a good description of these sciences would have a very great mirror for acquiring knowledge, since there is nothing in any of these sciences that does not bear the imprint of the Trinity."[11] That is, even philosophical knowledge contains truths about God the Father, Son, and Holy Spirit.

THEOLOGY'S PURPOSE: UNITY WITH GOD

A few years later Bonaventure returned to this important topic (i.e., the relationship of the liberal arts to theology) in his *On the Reduction of the Arts to Theology*. Zachary Hayes's summary is helpful: "In a mere seven pages ... Bonaventure argues concerning the relation of all forms of secular knowledge to the study of Scripture, or to theology. In doing so, he incorporates all the familiar and new forms of knowledge in the arts and sciences into an all-embracing, theological framework and integrates them into the journey of the human spirit into God."[12] In other words, one's knowledge—indeed, one's education—is disjointed and incomplete apart from the unifying and purposive structure provided by theology.

In the words of Bonaventure himself, "it is evident how the *manifold wisdom of God*, which is clearly revealed in sacred

Scripture, lies hidden in all knowledge and in all nature. It is clear also how all divisions of knowledge are servants of theology." Nonetheless, all of the sciences are given to humankind by God so that "faith may be strengthened, *God may be honored*, character may be formed, and consolation may be derived from union of the Spouse with the beloved, a union which takes place through charity."[13] According to Bonaventure theology sits at the head of the table, though that does not negate the value of the other arts for they too have important purposes. Most importantly, these arts, in service to theology, are ultimately for the purpose of human flourishing, that is, of uniting the student with the Master himself.

That is, after all, the ultimate purpose of the academic discipline of theology: to come to know God so as to be united with him. Theology's *telos*, as an academic area of study, is not just content mastery or domesticated axioms about God but personal communion with the triune God. For there is a reciprocity at work for the one who studies theology: the more she comes to know the object of her study (God himself), the more this God she knows gives his illuminating Holy Spirit to her so that she can know him more and more deeply. In the words of Mark McIntosh, "a mysterious affinity kindles between theology's object and theologians. As this happens, theologians start to catch glimpses of reality, shimmering and beckoning far beyond the proper frames and disciplines of theology itself."

This "shimmering" is vision of God himself, causing "theologians [to] find themselves tugged by the tide and tumbled by waves that delight and lure them deeper."[14] Theologians, in particular, get drawn without reserve into the subject of their study because, as it turns out, this *subject* is none other than God the Father, God the Son, and God the Holy Spirit. To study theology is to commune with God, and this truth alone is a powerful reason to seek a Christ-shaped liberal education.

THEOLOGY AND THE UNITY OF KNOWLEDGE

If Bonaventure is right, and theology is the queen of the sciences, then all of the other Christian liberal arts make sense only in reference to theology. Therefore, theology is not only one of the liberal arts, but it is *the* art among the liberal arts. In one sense this gives theology a primacy and pride of place in Christian education, in that it is "above" the other disciplines. In another sense it provides a unifying coherence which the other disciplines can seem, at times, to lack (as students often muse, "what does English 201 have to do with History of Philosophy 101 or Nursing 101?").

The reality in the twenty-first century is that curricula at most universities is dictated by accrediting agencies and a parent/student perspective that views the university economically. "How do I get the most bang for my buck?" which usually means, "how quickly can I graduate?" And, "can I take only those classes that are directly related to my major and my interests?" There is a fine line, it seems, between the historic trade schools and the modern university. Nonetheless, for a Christ-shaped liberal education the study of theology should and must take pride of place, given that it provides a coherence to all other areas of study. And such education must be sought where it may be found: at Christ-shaped liberal arts colleges.

Every student entering university must settle on a major, a focus of study. Some majors are intentionally designed to offer broad exposure to various disciplines. A degree in the liberal arts, for example, usually involves quite a number of classes in English, history, philosophy, and ancient and/or modern languages. Whereas other majors are, by necessity or by design, narrowly focused. A chemistry major will, of course, take most of her courses in the area of chemistry, whereas a pre-med degree will require some chemistry alongside biology, anatomy, and other health-field-related courses. On top of that there is invariably the requisite collection of non-major specific classes required by universities and accrediting agencies. In reviewing the lists of courses required for different degrees, it is worth asking: apart from a degree requirement or degree audit form, what holds all of this together? What is the cohesion of this plethora of disparate yet required courses? In Christ-shaped liberal education the answer is: theology. As the queen of the sciences, theology is the source and summit of the academic disciplines.

First, as the source, theology in its broadest sense is not only talk about God, but it is the understanding of God himself, as stated above. Because of that, everything that exists flows from the One who created all that there is and to whom all things will, ultimately, return. Christians confess, in the words of the Nicene Creed, to "believe in one God, the Father, the Almighty, creator of heaven and earth, of all that is, visible and invisible." In other words, God made the world and everything in it. Thus, every academic discipline that is dedicated to the study of the world (in the sense of the whole cosmos) and all that is in it (which is nearly every possible area of study) is, then, studying the creational act of God.

Creation itself teaches about God and is therefore theological. In the words of Basil of Caesarea, "the world was not devised at random or to no purpose, but to contribute to some useful end and to the great advantage of all beings, if it is truly a training place for rational souls and a school for attaining the knowledge of God."[15] Or, put slightly differently in the same homily, creation is "a place of training and a school for the souls of men."[16] Simply using our eyes to observe and appreciate creation is a kind of "doing" theology.

Theology is thus one of the first (if not *the* first) academic disciplines that every human being studies and practices. Who has not witnessed an infant begin to learn about the world around her, coming to realize her surroundings? Surely this helps to explain Jesus' own words: "at that time Jesus declared, 'I thank you, Father, Lord of heaven and earth, that you have hidden these things from the wise and understanding and revealed them to little children; yes, Father, for such was your gracious will'" (Matt. 11:25-26, ESV). As source, theology explains where everything comes from so that all areas of study (whether in the arts, liberal arts, sciences, etc.) are rooted in the creation of God. It is theology that provides all academic disciplines with their source of unity.

Second, as summit, all disciplines, if pursued rightly, return back to their theological grounding for God is the consummation of all things: "we have redemption through [Christ's] blood, the forgiveness of our trespasses, according to the riches of his grace, which he lavished upon us, in all wisdom and insight making known to us the mystery of his will, according to his purpose, which he set forth in Christ as a plan for the fullness of time, *to unite all things in him, things in heaven and things on earth*" (Eph. 1:7-10, ESV, emphasis added). If all things are united in God then that must include all knowledge, too. Thus, the end of all academic searching is relationship with God. God's creative act gives humankind the foundational "stuff" for our academic study (matter for the physicist and language for the poet, for example), and that "stuff" provides us with the material that we analyze and organize so that we come to know Godself.

THE SOURCE AND SUMMIT OF LEARNING

In the words of John Henry Newman, "All branches of knowledge are connected together, because the subject-matter of knowledge is intimately united in itself, as being the acts and the work of the Creator."[17] Thus, pursuing knowledge rightly brings the student-scholar into union with God. Knowledge for knowledge's sake often leads to academic idolatry and intellectual snobbery. Knowledge for God's sake leads to humility and charity as we are brought into intimate union with the One who is love (1 John 4:8). These observations inform the approach of Christ-shaped liberal education.

Not too long before his death in 1274 the great medieval theologian Thomas Aquinas gave a series of instructional sermons on the Apostle's Creed in which he wrote, "None of the philosophers before the advent of Christ with all of their striving were able to know so much of God and of those things required for [eternal] life as an old woman knows through faith after the coming of Christ."[18] What Thomas is saying is that theology, as knowledge of God, can be known by anyone, assuming they are a person of faith. In the modern university, the academic disciplines often are treated like self-contained silos of knowledge for, to echo the early Christian theologian Tertullian, what has Athens to do with Jerusalem?[19]

Outside of a Christian liberal arts setting there is often no attempt to seek after universal knowledge, in the sense that all academic disciplines have their source and summit in the person of God. In fact, many universities are no longer able to see the advantage of producing graduates who are generally educated, much less liberally educated. This makes a Christ-shaped liberal education the heartbeat, the *sine qua non*, of a Christian university. An assortment of theological courses does not make a university "Christian."

In selecting a college, then, there are compelling reasons to consider genuinely Christian schools, including especially Christian liberal arts colleges. Comparatively few students attend college to become professional theologians. Still, for Christ-shaped liberal education the mission is *not* only to graduate competent teachers, nurses, politicians, artists, social workers, etc. The mission is to graduate students who are fully aware that their chosen area of study and expertise, whatever that may be, leads them ultimately to a deeper relationship with God the Father, Son, and Holy Spirit: the source and summit of all that is.

1 John Henry Newman, *The Idea of a University* (New Haven: Yale University Press, 1996), 25.

2 Plato, *Republic* 379a.

3 Aristotle, *Metaphysics* 1000a.

4 Augustine of Hippo, *City of God* 8.1.

5 Origen of Alexandria, *Contra Celsum* 2.71.

6 Though non-monastic theologians still thought in these terms, such as Peter Lombard, *Sentences* Book I, Dist. I, c. 1-2.

7 Bernard McGinn, "*Regina quondam...*" *Speculum* 83 (2008): 832.

8 See Samuel Ijsseling, "The Liberal Arts and Education in the Middle Ages," in *Rhetoric and Philosophy in Conflict: An Historical Survey* (Dordrecht: Springer Netherlands, 1977).

9 Zachary Hayes, trans., *Works of St. Bonaventure, Volume XIV: Collations on the Seven Gifts of the Holy Spirit* (St. Bonaventure, NY: Franciscan Institute Publications, 2008), 87.

10 Ibid., 88.

11 Ibid., 92-93.

12 Zachary Hayes, *St. Bonaventure's On the Reduction of the Arts to Theology* (St. Bonaventure, NY: Franciscan Institute, 1996), 11.

13 Ibid., 61.

14 Mark McIntosh, *Divine Teaching: An Introduction to Christian Theology* (Malden, MA: Blackwell Publishing, 2008), 5.

15 Basil of Caesarea, "On the Hexaemeron" 1.6.

16 Ibid., 1.5.

17 Newman, *The Idea of a University*, 76.

18 Thomas Aquinas, "Collationes Credo in Deum" 1.

19 Tertullian, *Prescriptions against the Heretics* 7.

10

"OUR PLAY 'PLAYS' IN HIS PLAY"

*Delight, Instruction,
and the Performing Arts*

Timothy E. G. Bartel

THE PERFORMING ARTS, CHIEF AMONG THEM
theater, music, and dance, often seem to hang on the outskirts of
the liberal arts, never quite as central as studies like philosophy,
literature, and history. But the performing arts are in a sense
more immediate to everyday life than these disciplines. Most
people's days do not include the study of philosophy, but they
do often include listening to music, watching a TV show, or even
singing in the shower. If the liberal arts as a whole are concerned
with human flourishing, then the performing arts in particular

are especially concerned with that aspect of flourishing we call *delight*.

This idea that the performing arts exist for our delight goes all the way back to the ancients. The Roman poet Horace proposed that the goal of poetry is *simul et iucunda et idonea dicere vitae*, that is, "to delight and instruct in what is needful for life."[1] Poetry for the ancients included both epic storytelling and songwriting and theater. The ancient Greek philosophers Plato and Aristotle were two of the first authors to write about how poetry works. In the third book of Plato's *Republic*, Socrates explains:

> One kind of poetry and story-telling employs only imitation—tragedy and comedy as you say. Another employs only narration by the poet himself—you find this most of all in dithyrambs [short lyric poems]. A third kind uses both—as in epic poetry and many other places.[2]

Plato divides the types of poetry according to how they employ imitation. The imitation he has in mind here is "when [the poet] makes a speech as if he were someone else."[3] The distinction between stories that employ only imitation and those that don't may not seem terribly important, but it made all the difference in how the average Greek theater-goer experienced a poem. For epic and dithyrambic poems were read to the audience by a single reader, whereas tragic and comic poems were acted out on stage by multiple actors. These days we call such tragic and comic poems "drama," and they are the artistic ancestors of all contemporary theater, television, and film.

TRAGEDY

Plato's student Aristotle wrote a whole treatise, *Poetics*, focusing on ancient theater. Aristotle begins with the principle that all art is fundamentally imitative, and that imitation—along with the instruction and delight that come with it—is an instinct "lying deep in our nature." He explains:

> First, the instinct of imitation is implanted in man from childhood, one difference between him and other animals being that he is the most imitative of living creatures, and through imitation learns his earliest lessons; and no less useful is the pleasure felt in things imitated.[4]

Like his teacher, Aristotle divides the imitative art of poetry into four genres: epic, tragedy, comedy, and dithyrambic. But what he discusses most is tragedy: "Tragedy, then, is an imitation of an action that is serious, complete, and of a certain magnitude; ... in the form of action, not of narrative; through pity and fear effecting the proper purgation of these emotions."[5]

For Aristotle, the first and essential principle of tragedy is *action,* as opposed to narration. Most literary art—especially fiction and epic poetry—narrates its stories, but tragedy, and all theater by extension, embodies story through action. The primary vehicle of this action is the human body. In both ancient and modern theater, audiences experience the art form by watching, in real time, a human use their body to imitate the actions of a character. These actions involve speech, but they are not limited to speech. In fact, what distinguishes a good actor from a bad actor is often the wholehearted way in which they use their body—their posture, their facial expressions, their gait—to communicate their character, their emotions, and their decisions.

Tragedy for Aristotle also engages our emotions. Through an action that is "serious, complete, and of a certain magnitude," tragedy purges the "pity and fear" of the audience. This may become clearer if we look at the details of the tragic plot. The ideal plot of a tragedy, according to Aristotle, is one involving "a man who is not eminently good and just, yet whose misfortune is brought about not by vice or depravity, but by some error or frailty."[6] Characters like Harvey Dent in *The Dark Knight* or Anakin Skywalker in *Star Wars* are such men: motivated to do good, but, due to pain or poor judgement, falling into evil to accomplish their ends. Such characters and plots will stir both our pity and our fear, because "pity is aroused by unmerited misfortune, fear by the misfortune of a man like ourselves."[7]

It may be odd to think of experiencing pity and fear as a form of delight, but Aristotle seems to believe that the negative emotions we experience in tragedy allow us to deal with those emotions in a context that is relatively low stakes; the result is not ongoing despair, but a feeling of purification. To have worked through fear and pain into a feeling of peace—of *shalom* even— is to have practiced a deeply human activity: the catharsis of emotion. It is to have practiced inner growth, to have practiced maturation.

It might be helpful to pause and say that the dramatic theory of Aristotle that we have just explored is nearly the opposite of how many in contemporary culture treat the performing arts, especially television and music. Television and music are often treated as distractions, as amusements, as places to escape real life and to disengage from that which is taxing and troubling in the "real world." And to an extent, Aristotle agrees that the theater is different from the real world. It involves, after all, *imitated* action, *play* even. But what we learn from this play, according to Aristotle, has great value for what is most central to real life. I have often thought that what is wrong with American television is less a problem with the stories that are being told as with the approach of the audience. Too often audiences think of music or movies as products to be consumed, like a bag of snacks. Audiences chew through songs or TV episodes like handfuls of potato chips, and throw away the bag when finished. Plato, Aristotle, and Horace would rather we approach the performing arts as journeys to undertake.

We should not so much consume a piece of music or a tragic play as we should participate in it. One of the elements that is lost when music and theater are recorded is the powerful effect of a live audience. Actors and musicians in live performances are also *re*actors. An engaged audience who genuinely laughs at a joke and catches their breath at a betrayal lend an energy to the actors that is otherwise missing. Anyone who has ever tried to tell a joke or a story to a group of listeners will know what this is like. A bored listener makes for a frustrated storyteller; a fascinated listener makes for a confident storyteller. If we, as the audience, follow Aristotle's advice—if we are there, in part, for the emotional resonance and the emotional journey—the performance itself with be better. When audiences merely consume art and unthinkingly move on, artists are encouraged to make bad art.

TIME

One of the key elements that distinguishes the performing arts from visual arts like painting or sculpture is *time*. Music, dance, and theater require the passage of time in order for their art forms to work. While it is a good idea to take one's time perusing a painting, the whole painting is present to you in each moment. A sonata, a ballet, or a tragedy are never fully present all at once: they take time to experience in full. William Shakespeare meditated on time, most notably in one of his first and one of his last plays. In Shakespeare's early tragedy *Romeo and Juliet*, the Prologue states:

> The fearful passage of their death-marked love
>   And the continuance of their parent's rage—
> Which but their children's end, naught could re-
>   move—
> Is now the two hours' traffic of our stage;
> The which, if you with patient ears attend,
>   What here shall miss, our toil shall strive to
>   mend.[8]

— 117 —

The Prologue summarizes the story: the main characters' love, their parent's rage, and the tragic end of the lovers will proceed across the stage over the course of two hours. Shakespeare uses verbs that highlight the ongoing nature of their actions: "passage," "continuance," "traffic."

To be a member of the audience in *Romeo and Juliet* is to watch, and emotionally participate in, humans imitating actions that take some time to perform. But we are also promised that there is a time limit: eventually the lovers will die, which will remove the rage of their parents, and this will take place by the end of two hours. It is as if Shakespeare wants both to warn his audience about what they are about to experience, and to pull back the curtain on the art of writing tragedy: it is about creating, sustaining, and ending human action in and through time.

In one of his last plays, *A Winter's Tale*, Shakespeare personifies time itself as a character, and uses time's monologue as a transition point between acts:

> I that please some, try all; both joy and terror
> Of good and bad; that makes and unfolds error,
> Now take upon me in the name of Time
> To use my wings. It is not a crime
> To me or my swift passage that I slide
> O'er sixteen years and leave the growth untried
> Of that wide gap, since it is in my power
> To o'erthrow law, and in one self-born hour
> To plant and o'erwhelm custom.[9]

Time here describes itself as having power over law, custom, and even, in a sense, itself. This personified time can "slide / O'er sixteen years and leave the growth untried." It can, in other words, edit itself like the poet does.

The poet, who works in and with time, does not present events in time in the exact way they occur: the playwright presents to the audience the most important words and actions of each character in relation to the plot. If common experience of time's passage is a road, then the playwright hops us from section to section of road, sometimes forward, sometimes backward, sometimes leaving out, in Shakespeare's words, a "wide gap" of common time that was not relevant to the plot at hand. Thus, the creator of a piece of dramatic art shapes time like a sculptor shapes marble, and an essential part of the enjoyment of such art is our willing submission to the experience of time so shaped. This is why a piece of art like a play or a dance is always larger than we can ever grasp in one moment. We must—as we said before—take the time to go on a journey in order to experience it.

THE DRAMA OF THE GOSPEL

Thus far we have seen the heritage and basic shape of dramatic art: it is necessarily embodied and unfolds in time. Both the ancients and the moderns have seen dramatic art as an opportunity for delight, for catharsis, and even for gaining knowledge. But the performing arts as a whole have an even more specific relevance for the Christian. This is because the religion of Christianity centers around a story—the gospel—and much of what Christians are called to do involves studying and re-enacting this story.

Recent theologians have spoken of the gospel, and the gospel-centered Christian life, as fundamentally *dramatic*, and thus fundamentally concerned with embodied narrative and time. Kevin Vanhoozer writes: "Christian theology seeks to continue the way of truth and life, not by admiring it from afar, but by following and embodying it."[10] He explains:

> The Christian way is fundamentally dramatic, involving speech and action on behalf of Jesus's truth and life. It concerns a way of living truthfully, and its claim to truth cannot be isolated from the way of life

with which it is associated. For the way one lives *bodies forth* one's beliefs about the true, the good, and the beautiful ...

Thinking of doctrine in dramatic rather than theoretical terms provides a wonderfully engaging and integrative model for understanding what it means to follow—with all our mind, heart, soul, and strength—the way, truth, and life embodied and enacted in Jesus Christ.[11]

At the core of this passage is an important principle: "the way one lives bodies forth one's beliefs." How we spend our time, what we return to, what we practice, what we ignore: all these activities express something about what we hold to be valuable. The Christian life, then, far from being a dry mental exercise, is, according to Vanhoozer, best understood as an embodiment of belief. And this belief itself is about Jesus Christ, who himself "embodied and enacted" a saving "way, truth, and life."

It should not be surprising to us that Vanhoozer's phrase "bodies forth" is actually a quotation from Shakespeare's *A Midsummer's Night's Dream*:

THESEUS:

The poet's eye, in fine frenzy rolling,
Doth glance from heaven to earth, from earth to
    heaven;
And as imagination bodies forth
The forms of things unknown, the poet's pen
Turns them to shapes and gives to airy nothing
A local habitation and a name.[12]

For Shakespeare's Athenian Duke Theseus, the imagination "bodies forth ... airy nothing" and turns it, through the poet's pen, into something that seems real, with "a local habitation and a name." Theseus's words about poetic imagination may be beautifully put, but his overall attitude is negative. What seems to be real in poetry is, in fact, nothing. But Shakespeare gives a wiser character the final say in the matter:

HIPPOLYTA:

But all the story of the night told over ...
More witnesseth than fancy's images
And grows to something of great constancy;
But, howsoever, strange and admirable.[13]

For Hippolyta, some stories can achieve truth, can grow to "something of great constancy" while being still "strange and admirable."

This, I would argue, is what the Christian story can be: strange, admirable, constant, and bodied forth in the acting out of the gospel in each individual life. We began this chapter by suggesting that the performing arts feature more prominently in our everyday experience than do other liberal arts. We now see that the performing arts are present even in the acting out and sharing of our faith. Further, they can inform how we think of the object of our faith: the drama that is the gospel.

The theologian Hans Urs Von Balthasar argues that our lives—how we live them, what we reveal through our actions—should be seen in the context of a story that God himself is telling: "our play 'plays' in his play."[14] In the incarnation of Christ, Von Balthasar explains, "on the human stage he 'plays' through human beings and ultimately *as* a human being."[15] Here Balthasar alludes not to Shakespeare but to the Victorian English poet Gerard Manley Hopkins, who wrote that man

Acts in God's eye what in God's eye he is:
Christ. For Christ plays in ten thousand places,
Lovely in limbs and lovely in eyes not his
To the Father through the features of men's faces.[16]

Hopkins is famous for his dizzying wordplay, and here he is at his finest in describing Christ's active presence in human affairs, as well as his role as mediator between God and man. But Von Balthasar would have us remember that Christ's activity is not a mere shadowy imitation of man: Christ became human—the Word became flesh—taking on, in a sense, the ultimate dramatic role: to truly become one's character, even to the point of death.

THE WORTH OF THE STAGE

To so characterize the gospel and the Christian life is, of course, to make a metaphor. Although the gospel and our life in response to it are not literal plays acted on stages, the strong resemblances between the two do warrant a detailed metaphor. Far from making our little human dramas insignificant, the metaphor of God as divine playwright and human actor imbues the art of drama with great potential. Here is Balthasar again:

> In the theater the man attempts a kind of transcendence, endeavoring both to observe and to judge his own truth, in virtue of a transformation—through the dialectic of the concealing-revealing mask—by which he tries to gain clarity about himself. Man himself beckons, invites the approach to a revelation about himself.[17]

It is through the stage, and the performances that take place upon it, that humans can come to better understand themselves, and, by analogy, God. The performing arts, then, turn out to fit into the liberal arts in general as another important path to self-knowledge, and thus, further flourishing. This is the second half of Horace's dictum about poetry we saw above: art is both for delight and for *instruction*. And the instruction of theater, according to Balthasar, comes as a revelation in the midst of performance.

Each liberal art is intrinsically valuable inasmuch as it leads us to wisdom, that same wisdom that the author of Proverbs says, "cries aloud in the streets." In the introduction of this book, we saw how the liberal arts as a whole are "Christ-shaped." This is more than slapping a Christian label on a non-Christian idea. For one of the core doctrines of the Old Testament is that wisdom — the wisdom of God himself — is fundamental to the nature and workings of the universe.

When humans discover and follow this wisdom, they shape themselves into beings who live in proper relationship and harmony with the universe. In philosophical terms, we might say that *ethics* is based in *ontology*. In other words, the way we should act, the way we should live, is based on how the created universe works. Those behaviors we call *good* and those behaviors we call *evil*, those behaviors that lead to human flourishing and those behaviors that lead to human destruction, are not random; they are related to the very fabric of existence, a fabric woven by God the Word in the beginning of all things. If any academic study is to be worthwhile, then, it must take into account that fabric of existence and our place within it. To justify any art or science merely by the fact that it can get one a good job, or make money, is not enough. Because the universe is Christ-shaped, because the universe is Christ-oriented, all studies of enduring worth will also, ultimately, be Christ-shaped and Christ-oriented. At the end of time, we will not stand before a judge who asks us how practical our career choices were, or whether our college major led to a high-paying job. The Judge we will stand before is the cosmos-creating God, and his commandments are much more fundamental: *get wisdom*, and *love the Lord thy God.*

How do the performing arts fit into these ultimate commandments? The performing arts are a distinctly *practical* path to wisdom, in that they involve the physical movements of the human body, patterned in those ways that communicate beauty, goodness, and truth. The performing arts remind us that we are created as embodied creatures. And these bodies that we have been given are not for mere animal pleasures or instinctual living, but for bodying forth, for incarnating, the patterns of life that lead to virtue and right relationship with the earth, with our fellow humans, and with God. These truths have been recognized from the ancient world to the present, and those who choose to pursue a study of the performing arts will be rewarded with not just a new appreciation for an art form, but with new revelations about life itself, a flourishing life grounded in the wisdom and the love of God.

---

[1] Horace, *Satires. Epistles. The Art of Poetry* (Cambridge, MA: Harvard University Press, 1926), 478.

[2] Plato, *The Republic* 394c.

[3] Ibid., 393b.

[4] Aristotle, *Poetics* 1446b, 5-10.

[5] Ibid., 1449b. 21-28.

[6] Ibid., 1453a. 7-9.

[7] Ibid., 1453a. 5-7.

[8] Shakespeare, "Romeo and Juliet," in *The Oxford Shakespeare* (Oxford: Oxford University Press, 2005), Prologue, 9-14.

[9] Shakespeare, "A Winter's Tale," in *The Oxford Shakespeare*, 4.1.1-9.

[10] Kevin Vanhoozer, *The Drama of Doctrine: A Canonical-Linguistic Approach to Christian Theology* (Louisville, KY: Westminster John Knox, 2005), 15.

[11] Ibid., 15-16.

[12] Shakespeare, "A Midsummer's Night's Dream," in *The Oxford Shakespeare*, 5.1.13-18.

[13] Ibid., 5.1.24, 2-28.

---

[14] Hans Urs Von Balthasar, *Theo-Drama: Theological Dramatic Theory*, Vol. 1: *Prolegomena* (San Francisco: Ignatius, 1988), 19.

[15] Ibid., 20.

[16] Gerard Manley Hopkins, *Mortal Beauty, God's Grace: Major Poems and Spiritual Writings* (New York: Vintage, 2003), 21.

[17] Balthasar, *Theo-Drama*, 12.

11

CAN A B.A. IN LIBERAL STUDIES GET ME A JOB?

John Mark Reynolds

WHAT DOES IT PROFIT A PERSON TO GAIN A JOB and lose happiness? The proper college degree will help you gain both a job and happiness: do well by doing good.

Consider the question whether a degree in liberal studies—whether via Christ-shaped liberal education or not—can ensure employment. The truth is that no major, no education "can get" you or me a job. This is because the future is uncertain. Revolutionary change can sweep away the old rules in an instant: if you prepared to work for the Soviet system at the University of Moscow in 1988, you were obsolete in 1989. Liberal arts education does not try to guess what the world will be like decades from now, when a freshman today is at the height of his or her career. Instead, a liberal arts education focuses on what has always been needed, guessing that if one has need of a skill to succeed in the years 1719, 1819, 1919, and 2019, those skills will still be needed in thirty years!

WHAT IS A COLLEGE DEGREE FOR?

As Jeffrey and Loftin indicate in chapter four, the institution of college grew out of a Christian desire to seek the good, truth, and beauty. Young men (and sadly it would be years before women were involved) got training to become *gentlemen*. This began as a purely class distinction, but times changed. Being a "gentleman" became as much or more about behavior.[1] A gentleman acted with virtue, fit to lead. When a wealthy family sent a son to college, they anticipated he would become a *man*.

Some job training was involved, of course: lawyers, ministers, and medical doctors required training in order to enter the three leading professions of Christendom. The training was intense, but college also wanted these men to be *gentlemen*. Nobody wanted a lawyer, pastor, or doctor who was a cad!

The central focus of college was not, however, getting a job. The central focus, rather, was cultivating a certain way of living. At best, this was the cultivation of virtue. As for most jobs outside the professions, apprenticeships and family connections did most of the work. A college degree might even be an impediment. There is a reason that when I was a boy the old board game "Life" made skipping college a shortcut to "business," and the choice was not viewed as irrational. After all, right into the early 1950's, Harry S. Truman occupied the White House with no college diploma. John D. Rockefeller, the fabulously wealthy, self-made oil tycoon, helped fund and found a university in Chicago, although he never graduated from one himself.

Despite garnering increased job training responsibilities after World War II (1945), the college retained its first role: creating a leadership class for the Republic. Government subsidies added to the college mission substantially and this changed what working class people needed to do: high school and college became, in part, the new union card, a ticket to access jobs.

Nursing, for example, moved from training in a hospital to a baccalaureate program in a college. Training for the *job* in a college (away from a hospital) may have been unnecessary—alternative models were available—but the addition (in many liberal arts colleges) of a strong liberal arts education was a great benefit. Every patient hopes his nurse, a highly trained medical professional, is also trained in the humane arts!

College was not, perhaps, the most efficient way to do more expansive job training, but the growth of "practical" majors at liberal arts colleges all over the nation did expose more students to training in virtue. Sadly, some of these schools abandoned their old liberal arts mission to double down on the practical, while others allowed the liberal arts to become a confused mess of multiple majors and cafeteria courses. You can get a good meal in a cafeteria, but only with planning. In the same way, you can choose good classes out of a catalog if you get good guidance. Fortunately, more than a few liberal arts colleges kept a strong core of classes that retained training in virtue. This was particularly true in Christian colleges.

Most colleges retained some of the old mission of training good leaders alongside the new task of job training. There is often a tension between these tasks, though, which results in time-wasting, shallow liberal arts classes combined with job training classes that could have been more efficiently done in industry or without the distraction of other coursework. This is hardly ideal.

THE SOUL OF CHRIST-SHAPED LIBERAL EDUCATION

The pure liberal arts major refuses to accept the bloat and the tension that developed in the twentieth century college. She wants instead what Theodore Roosevelt got: mentoring at an excellent liberal arts college. She might be seen by some as operating at a disadvantage. After all, the student who declares this year's favorite "practical" major is getting some liberal arts *and* a clear career track. Yet, surprisingly, the end result is that the liberal arts major finds herself in a strong practical position. Not doing job training (directly) turns out to be excellent job training, as many companies have discovered.[2] Before looking at the evidence that this is true and why it is so, we must pause and remind ourselves of one thing: done properly, a liberal arts major has human value and, after all, there is no profit in gaining the world and losing the soul.

No Christian thinks a person is valued by financial worth, otherwise Jesus was a relative failure! Jesus, of course, did not go to college, not even the educational system of his day. Doesn't that mean that a liberal arts education, often expensive, is unnecessary?

A liberal arts education is *not* necessary to wisdom. A bad liberal arts education may even deter finding wisdom, if it deters the fear of the Lord which is the beginning of wisdom. Done properly, however, Christ-shaped liberal education will aid a willing student in learning to be a lady or a gentleman: a person of character ready to serve others. My car will run without air conditioning, but in Houston the trip is better, much more tolerable, if the air conditioning works. In fact, a dead air conditioner might keep many Houstonians from a road trip if it's July! A person *can* get what a liberal arts education provides without college, but it is uncomfortably difficult and most of us will not bother.

A good liberal arts education starts with Socrates' charge to "know yourself," and part of that knowing, in his day and our own, is seeing our relative smallness. We are not much compared to the cosmos and (especially) God. When a person sees, through careful study of both ideas and nature, the glory of God, then he or she is humbled. God is great.

Our humility begins in seeing what we are compared to God, but it does not end with God. A liberal arts student soon learns to be humbled by the vast extent of human art, culture, and knowledge. I have spent years thinking about the meaning of Plato's *Republic* and have yet to reach an end. When I turn to consider all of ancient Greek culture, I am overwhelmed with what there is to learn. Then I look at First Nations and the wisdom found in those cultures here in America, or English history, or the complex glories to be found in the Indian sub-culture. As a Christian, I wonder about one of the first Christian lands, Aksum.

A Christ-shaped liberal education makes a person penitent, because we see the goodness of God and our own inadequacy. We are not what we hope to be. Humility in the face of God, seeing God's endless beauty, truth, and goodness shows us that we can learn, world without end. College sets us up for Paradise: we recover the lost tools of eternal learning. The liberal arts education instills deeper literacy, critical reasoning skills, and some depth of knowledge about the home culture.

Finally, a good liberal arts education rejects the modern tendency to turn learning into a commodity and centers its processes instead around the relationship of a mentor and a student. The curriculum is what a student needs to develop (or at least to understand) courage, moderation, prudence, and practical wisdom. The Christian liberal arts college provides a guide to hope, faith, and love as the greatest virtues.

On its own a book cannot make you virtuous, but you can learn about virtue from a book and practice that virtue under the guidance of a good teacher in a small community. Because this community centers on texts, artifacts, art, and oral history, *the dead are not dead to us*. The living community dialogs with those who have gone before them in history and applies past wisdom (or folly!) to present questions.

If a student can find a Socrates or Jesus, they should follow him. Such genius in history is rare, however, and few of us will study under the equivalent of such teachers. Instead, Christ-shaped liberal education seeks out *decent* mentors for us. If the teachers individually are not Socrates, then it must also be remembered that the students are rarely Plato (his greatest student). For the Christian liberal arts college (as most were historically in North American and Europe), the hope is that Christ within each professor will, on the whole, allow for Christian mentoring. When a Christian liberal arts education is working, the disciples of Jesus walk with younger disciples of Jesus and Christ within is made evident to all: full of grace and truth.

THE PRACTICAL WORTH OF LIBERAL STUDIES

Given an academic's tendency to study things, it's not surprising that the value of a liberal arts education itself has been studied. The result is conclusive: a liberal arts degree is monetarily valuable.[3] In sum, a liberal arts education helps a graduate get a job and improves his or her economic prospects. This is not surprising since liberal arts majors have honed three perennially marketable skills: reading well, writing well, and thinking well. Add in numeracy and the liberal arts major is well prepared for a diversity of careers.

Why prepare for a diversity of careers, though, instead of doggedly focusing your preparation on a single career plan? Studies show that less than one third of people end up actually working in their majors.[4] According to the Department of Labor's Bureau of Labor Statistics, the average worker has ten different jobs before the age of 40.[5] In fact, most of us will have as many as seven different *careers* over a lifetime.[6] Besides, trying in four years of one's late teens and early twenties to gain the *specific* skills necessary for a certain job is all but impossible. Even the most specialized of majors will require a lifetime of on-the-job training to keep current in the field. In most jobs (ask a human resource manager), new hires with the ability to learn will master the job as they earn. The liberal arts major has lifetime skills, and this may be one reason they are not as likely to be unemployed.[7] It is the mental flexibility that is featured in liberal arts education—and not learning skills that often become antiquated in a few years—that exactly fits the workplace.

Think about the future. If you are starting college at 18, you will end your career more than fifty years from now. What will the economy look like in 50 years? Take any year from American history more than 50 fifty years ago and do a search for predictions about the economy from that year. You will find that the predictions almost always were wrong. For example, I graduated from college in 1986, having majored in religion and philosophy. That did not seem very practical, but then the future was not going to look like the past. You can see this for yourself by comparing the Fortune 500 list from 1986 to that of 2019.[8] I graduated in upstate New York where practical parents would have steered me toward Kodak (33 on the 1986 list) or Xerox (40) as safe corporate bets. Kodak, so powerful in Rochester it then was called the "Great Yellow Mother" for the color of the company film boxes and the security of jobs, is today a shadow of itself and doesn't even appear on the 2019 list. Xerox is now 318th. Meanwhile, though no one then realized it, investing in Apple or looking into the company Sam Walton was running (Walmart) would have been a good idea.[9]

Meanwhile, the dawn of the internet disrupted a great many plans (even Microsoft bobbled that change[10]). Everyone faced change: education, which seemed insulated from the online revolution, wasn't. If you were teaching at the time, the differences could be frightening ("This is not what my practical credential taught me!") or exhilarating. Fortunately, the liberal arts education I'd received helped me anticipate key changes, and so by the late 1980s I was experimenting with teaching philosophy on a Commodore 64 via a service called Q-link (you'll probably need to Google those). The point is that my liberal arts education helped me adapt and even lead in education.

By focusing on the enduring things, the liberal arts major knows what does not endure. The educational practice of the 1980s did not account for the internet, because there was no internet. The world was bound to change as the world always has, but establishments, the most practical folk, are built to last.

Human nature, however, did not change with the coming of the internet. Humans still needed to read well, write well, think well, and be mentored into virtue.

Social media does not make it less necessary to be kind or more wrong to be cruel. We have new tools to be ourselves and are less able to hide the people we are, but we have not changed. The *abilities* to do good and evil are greater, but the desires remain merely human. We are neither in the best of times nor the worst of times: we are in every time since Adam and Eve left Eden.

The great folly is to try to guess *change*. Things change in unexpected ways, and the colleges that sell you today's practical major are really marketing *what would have worked* if you had graduated twenty years ago. They are, in other words, selling you today's jobs based on present trends—but you will live decades longer (God willing) than today's jobs may exist. If a college were great at such predictions, they would not need to charge you tuition. They could simply bet on the future in the stock market or by investing in startups.

AN ETERNAL RESPONSE

A college cannot be sure what the economy will look like by the middle of your career, but you can be certain that Paradise will be shalom. God deals with different peoples in their own languages and in the images that will work for them. Yet God as God does not change. College, you recall, was created to look for the eternal. The *highest* education looks to God, since the eternal truth, the deepest beauty, and goodness never change.

Imagine a river. The water is always flowing. As the Greek philosopher Heraclitus noted, we cannot step in the same river twice. Though the water changes, we cannot step into *exactly* the same river that our friend experienced yesterday (different water!). Yet the name of the river has not changed. If we are swimming the Little Sandy today, we do not think this is a *totally* different river from yesterday. The banks of the river are (more or less) the same. Something endures from day to month to year to century. In an old river, like the Nile in Egypt, we think that *this* river is (in one sense) the same river on which Cleopatra sailed. Christ-shaped liberal education looks for the banks—that is, the idea—of the river and does not merely collect some of today's water and dole it out to students. The water, of course, keeps flowing. But if we know the place, shape, and idea of the river, then we can always find the water. A liberal arts education, with a focus on enduring art, oral tradition, folk wisdom, artifacts, and literature, shows us where good water often has been found.

Perhaps most practically, the one thing all of us humans can be sure we will do is die. This fact is seldom included in college brochures, because, as life insurance salespeople know, nobody likes preparing for death or even admitting they will die. Colleges bent on *selling* education (with lots of debt!) as a commodity will ignore the fact that one (albeit not the only) job of education is to prepare us for a good death. Eternity awaits us, and no amount of cash, no fame, and no power on Earth prepares us for eternity.

We will die. Everyone *knows* this, but few of us think about it. Why? If death is the end, then we need not consider death as part of our behavior. Death, so the thinking goes, ends everything. Yet compelling reasons and evidence suggest that death is not the end, and if this is so then preparing for the afterlife is necessary. Christianity does not take the fact of death to imply that this life does not matter. To the contrary, we know that this life is joyful and valuable for its own sake. So, a good education would make us fit for this life while preparing us for the life to come. Christ-shaped liberal education is designed to do this very thing: make human life whole, from conception to death.

Nobody can learn without *desire,* a form of love. We see beauty in art and feel love. We see the glory of the stars and feel love. We see an elegant proof in logic and can feel love. Something good, beautiful, and true proves love. This love drives us to know and so achieve genuine education. Love endures, never failing. Love is the fuel to drive us toward the Good. We desire and so we work, and by grace through faith, God meets our need.

Nothing and no one but the eternal God can meet the deep desire beauty stirs in our souls. If this is so, then a *liberal arts education* is necessary to health. We want something deeper than jobs, and if we are not given hope of gaining that, the Beloved, we will despair.

A good, Christ-shaped liberal arts education probably (almost surely) will help one to get a good job, but most vitally it will point one to the Love that moves the heavens and the furthest stars.

---

[1] The novels of Anthony Trollope chart the change. See his Barchester series as a starting place. These are great fun to read!

[2] For just one example, see Sydney Johnson, "As Tech Companies Hire More Liberal Arts Majors, More Students Are Choosing STEM Degrees," *Ed-Surge*, November 13, 2018, <https://www.edsurge.com/news/2018-11-13-as-tech-companies-hire-more-liberal-arts-majors-more-students-are-choosing-stem-degrees>.

[3] Such studies have been performed many times, in fact. One excellent example is "The Economic Benefits and Costs of a Liberal Arts Education," published by the Andrew W. Mellon Foundation in January 2019, is available at < https://mellon.org/news-blog/articles/economic-benefits-and-costs-liberal-arts-education/#top>.

[4] Brad Plumer, "Only 27 percent of college grads have a job related to their major," *The Washington Post*, May 20, 2013, < https://www.washingtonpost.com/news/wonk/wp/2013/05/20/only-27-percent-of-college-grads-have-a-job-related-to-their-major/>.

[5] https://www.bls.gov/news.release/pdf/nlsoy.pdf.

[6] https://careers-advice-online.com/career-change-statistics.html.

[7] See, for example, Derek Newton, "It's Not Liberal Arts and Literature Majors Who Are Most Underemployed," *Forbes*, May 31, 2018, < https://www.forbes.com/sites/dereknewton/2018/05/31/its-not-liberal-arts-and-literature-majors-who-are-most-underemployed/#4fc2b48111de> and Michael S. Roth, "The Liberal Arts Are Marketable," *The Wall Street Journal*, September 4, 2017, < https://www.wsj.com/articles/the-liberal-arts-are-marketable-1504549779>.

[8] https://archive.fortune.com/magazines/fortune/fortune500_archive/full/1986/ versus https://fortune.com/fortune500/search/.

[9] https://www.investopedia.com/articles/active-trading/080715/if-you-would-have-invested-right-after-apples-ipo.asp.

[10] https://www.extremetech.com/computing/206519-microsoft-saw-the-future-but-missed-creating-it.

INDEX

Made in the USA
Columbia, SC
15 November 2022

71188825R00093